SHELLEY

Poetry & Prose

AMS PRESS
NEW YORK

PERCY BYSSHE SHELLEY
From a painting made at Rome in 1819 by Miss Curran

S H E L L E Y

Poetry & Prose

With Essays by

BROWNING, BAGEHOT, SWINBURNE

And Reminiscences by Others

With an Introduction and Notes by

A. M. D. HUGHES

OXFORD

AT THE CLARENDON PRESS

Library of Congress Cataloging in Publication Data

Shelley, Percy Bysshe, 1792–1822.
  Shelley.

  Reprint of the 1931 ed. published by Clarendon
Press, Oxford.
  I. Hughes, Arthur Montague D'Urban, 1873-
PR5403.H8   1980   821'.7   76-29404
ISBN 0-404-15323-2

MANUFACTURED
IN THE UNITED STATES OF AMERICA

CONTENTS

CONTENTS

SELECTIONS (*contd.*)

INTRODUCTION

SHELLEY has written in his *Hymn to Intellectual Beauty* and in the dedicatory verses to *The Revolt of Islam* of luminous moments in his life at Eton, when he conceived his ruling passion. In one of these, hearing from the playground the familiar noise of the bully and the victim in the near school-room, he had vowed with tears to live contending with the oppressors of his kind, and to be 'wise and just and free and mild'; and in another a 'shadow' touched him of the Power to which all his poetry is an oblation—the One Spirit manifested in nature's beauty and in man's love. These intimations he soon began to think out with the aid of the two minds which of all others were to govern him, for he read, as it seems, before leaving school the *Symposium* of Plato and the *Political Justice* of William Godwin. It was in the Greek master that he found, as time went on, the abettor of his deeper thought and greater poetry, for the heart of Shelley's 'prophecy' is an impassioned Platonism in the terms of life and love, and even the shorter lyrics are coloured with the philosophy in which his keenest feeling ended or began. All the joy and pain, his own or others', that burdened his poetry appeared to him to be taking place in a cosmic drama proceeding through all time in the natural world, in political societies, and in the hearts of men. In that great action the Spirit of Beauty and Good, interfused with the things of sense, with the sullen matter of nature, or the carnal element in man, moulds them, 'as each mass may bear', to its own likeness; sometimes prevails upon them 'in its glory and its might'; sometimes seems to weary or fail. And according to his mood he looks forward in his imaginations to the victory of the Spirit in all its spheres—to a perfected humanity on a planet where there shall be no rigorous clime, nor any anger in beast or bird, nor poison in herb or tree ; or he takes his theme from the *Symposium* or the *Phaedo*— the spirit pining in the bonds of time, the 'hidden want' in the perishable beauty or the earthly love, life an exile, and death the recall. Between these views he is always wavering ; but the more he knew of the mystery of failure and pain, the oftener he turned from Godwin to Plato, from the issue in society at large to that in his own soul, from the subject of the earthly paradise to that of the spiritual fulfilment in 'a world far from ours'.

It was some time, however, before the Platonic philosophy took hold, and meanwhile he threw himself into the hope and thought of the Revolution, as presented in the serene audacity of *Political Justice*. Godwin had there contended that the modern Church and State, and a host of fallacies incorporate with them, were the roots of all the evil among men ; but that reason, so sadly inclined to take its ply from circumstances, and to be thwarted by the faiths and customs of its own instituting, might at length rise up, slowly at first, then perhaps swiftly and mightily, and cast these shackles from it ; and thereupon create in all the world societies unstained by war and crime, where the utmost of human power should ripen, and a man should be his own governor, and all authority at point of vanishing. That Shelley gave his mind to this book is not wonderful ; for the preposterous theory was argued with a logical architecture, and instinct with a moral sense that moved him, as he told its author, for the first time 'really to think and feel'. Not only did it seem to him 'the first moral system explicitly founded on the negativeness of rights and the positiveness of duties', but the first to conceive worthily of human nature, for the perfect humanity which the prophets saw in dreams Godwin beheld in prospect, with here and there a glowing interval in his placid style : 'There will be no disease, no anguish, no melancholy, and no resentment, but every man will seek with ineffable ardour the good of all.' It is not a little owing to this treatise that hope always fought with sadness in Shelley's spirit and sang its antiphon in his poetry. And to some extent the complexion of his own mind was here reflected, where all was enchantment, yet all was reason. For neither the poet nor the reformer in him ever parted from the theorist. He wrote of himself with truth as

> a nerve o'er which do creep
> The else unfelt oppressions of this earth;

and his friends noted in his face and bearing, what all men may in his poetry, the same extreme of ardour as of delicacy. But the blood called to the brain; the brain replied with its own daring; and positive and explicit thought was the fruit or food of the passion. He poured, therefore, his own spirit of expectation into the syllogisms of *Political Justice*. Wordsworth also, in one of his revolutionary phases, had found in Godwin's argument his rock. It 'fixed the hopes of man for ever in a clearer element', and in the day of disappointment comforted the mind with ideal certainty, like the 'clear synthesis built up aloft' of a geometric proof. Shelley took it, at least in the earlier years, in another way. As he abounded in the imagination of exultant power without let or limit—the 'tamelessness', for instance, of wind, or water, or fire—so he loved to think of waves of spiritual energy, sudden and mighty, purging hearts and renewing all things. To him the Godwinian demonstration was rather like the shell in *Prometheus Unbound*, at the blast of which all men and creatures put away their evil properties. It had somehow lost its power since its maker first blew it in 1793, but the magic only slumbered and might be re-awaked.

Shelley left Eton in the summer of 1810; and his subsequent life divides into two periods—before and after his departure for Italy in the spring of 1818, one of nearly eight years, the other of more than four. The first was a time of precipitate adventure, when by word and deed he 'tried the force of reason' on the principles, religious and social, of the society around him, with bitter consequences to others and 'strange defeatures' in himself. 'With fine affections and aspirations gone all such a road—A man infinitely too weak for that solitary climbing of the Alps which he undertook in spite of all the world—A haggard existence that of his!' So wrote Carlyle, and so thought, no doubt, the charitable onlooker in Shelley's day. But the charitable are too few; and one of the purest-hearted of men came to feel that he was regarded by all but a few friends as a being 'whose look even might infect'. That he should have seen no fault of his own in these calamities is impossible; but he was so tempered as to perceive much more clearly the obduracy of the world. And of one thing he never doubted—his purposes had been high and pure, and his message in the main true. The poems written in England, except *Alastor*, ring the changes on the same theme of liberty, and the splendid enterprise of its martyrs, and its well-spring in the heart of youth. Nevertheless, a deepening culture and the lesson of the facts were changing him, and in Italy the change was fulfilled. He had now a respite from his fierce controversies, and, though still a soldier of the Revolution, was lightlier engaged; and his genius burned within him in the prospect of the storied cities and the sunlit mountains and seas. Moreover, it was in this period that he came to 'diet', as he once put it, on the Greek poets and the dialogues of Plato. In these fostering airs his mind soon teemed with its finest fruits, and put forth powers which had not till then appeared. He now desisted from his crude romances of political martyrdom, and in this new phase of his poetry the good cause in society took its place in an outer sphere of the great contention of good and evil, life and death, of which the burning centre was his own soul. Nor could he well hold on to his credulous Godwinism where all things spoke to him of the succession of great ages, each with its gain and loss and its splendour and decline. In *Prometheus Unbound*, written in the first two years in Italy, the day of man's perfection comes about in no place or time, but in idea, and concomitantly with a new earth and heaven. When, again, the Revolution actually renewed itself in Spain, Naples, Greece, and Shelley hailed it in his choric odes and in *Hellas*, the theme of his song was not the millennial ecstasy, but the great memories of the insurgent peoples and the enlarging river of will and thought. It was even good for Shelley's poetry that his hope could falter. The last chorus of *Hellas* closes what may be called in a large sense the political verse on the most poignant and inward of its notes, where a sudden thought breaks the wings of his jubilance, and it falls and dies in a tired longing.

But Shelley wrote his best when his primary theme is not the new age, but himself. All his themes are indeed, in a word of his own, 'interfluous'; but it is easy to distinguish a line of longer poems from *Queen Mab* to *Prometheus Unbound*, and thence to *Hellas*, and another line from *Alastor* to *Epipsychidion* and *Adonais* and *The Triumph of Life*, where he explores the spiritual world and becomes a poet of the first and last things. It was here that he plumbed most deeply the conception of the Intellectual Beauty and its inconstant potency, the power which by turns we have and want, and cannot have and hold. For he is more particularly the poet of sorrow. Even in the quieter years in Italy sorrow was still constant to him: in the 'hunt of obloquy', now at greater distance, but all the while in cry; in the deaths of two of his children; and in an increasing sense of a wrongness in his own life and in the world. Men had answered his devotion to them with hate; love itself, as it seemed by its very nature, 'seeking in a mortal image the

likeness of what is, perhaps, eternal', had filled his life with
pain. Often as he might feel himself 'in love with easeful
Death', no poet has brooded on the outrage of death more
intently; nor did he ask in vain for a portion of Dante's
spirit in the pageant of enthralling desire which was his last
labour.[1] These are the main burdens of his 'metaphysical'
poetry—his parables, visions, elegies, and the unmatchable
lyrics, of which many a one has distilled his melancholy in a
handful of notes. But he may be said to have lived by insur-
rection; and the man 'falling on the thorns of life' is anon
the fiery will which can rest in nothing but perfect freedom
and the infinite of joy. There is surely no keener and no
more plangent music of the heart's desire than in those
poems where Shelley wrote of an earthly paradise, or of the
country of the soul beyond this scene of dying beauty and
failing love. But then his mood changes, and he seeks the
rapture and the release, not fugitively, in a grove of the
blest, but in the battle of his time, if the Power that moves
in the autumn wind, cleansing and fertilizing, will 'be
through his mouth to unawakened earth the trumpet of
a prophecy'. Indeed, whatever the mood—dejection, or
'immortal longing', or 'clear keen joyance'—it is always the
passion for life; a passion which, though it dreamed so often
of a world too bright for the plainness of things, was more
and more conversant with the reality which had called it
forth. Shelley lived eagerly, with an intense enjoyment of
landscape and travel, a boat or a yacht, the company of his
friends, and many homely pleasures; and he was casually
a shrewd observer. Much of his intercourse was with men of
action and men of the world, and he looked with a beating
heart on the drama of great affairs. All this side of him
appeared in his art, or inclined him to adventures in it, in his
latter years: in the familiar verse of *Julian and Maddalo* or

[1] *The Triumph of Life.*

A Letter to Maria Gisborne—perhaps the most exquisite of
its kind; in the fragments of tales after Byron or Keats;
in political and literary satire ; and in the drama of *The Cenci*,
which recovered the touch of the old masters like nothing
else since Massinger and Ford. And the experiments in the
art are as many as in the matter. But the masterpiece
that should have called up all his powers was never written.

There is hardly another great poet of whom it may be said
as truly that he comes home only to readers of certain kinds.
He is provocative of many censures, and great authorities
have pressed them. 'The author of the *Prometheus Unbound*',
wrote Hazlitt, 'has a fire in his eye, a fever in his blood, a
maggot in his brain, a hectic flutter in his speech, which
mark out the philosophic fanatic. . . . As is often observable
in the case of religious enthusiasts, there is a slenderness of
constitutional *stamina*, which renders the flesh no match for
the spirit. His bending, flexible form appears to take no
strong hold of things, does not grapple with the world
about him, but slides from it like a river.' 'Pallid and
hysterical,' says Carlyle. Peacock thought that he might
have lived to kill his poetry with despondence, 'passing his
days like Volney, looking on the world from his windows
without taking part in its turmoils, and perhaps like the same
or some other great apostle of liberty . . . desiring that nothing
should be inscribed on his tomb but his name, the dates of
his birth and death, and the single word, 'DÉSILLUSIONNÉ.'

Other critics level at his art, and point to his *Defence of
Poetry* as an index both of its strength and weakness. For
the theme of that bold and beautiful essay is the struggle of
Spirit and Matter, whether in the moral history of the race
or the poet's operation on words. The One Spirit of beauty
and good, which brings the healthful order or 'rhythm' into
every phase of life, attains to its highest intensity in poetry,
which is therefore the mark and measure, the seed and fruit

of the general happiness. But neither in its work upon society, nor when in the poet's mind it grapples with the subject and the means of expression, can the fitful fire entirely penetrate the mass. The mysterious unbidden inspiration is never quite translated in the words and rhythms, and 'when composition begins is already on the wane'. Shelley, while there was still time, would pour his words on paper, and put in the repairs and supplements when 'the thing had gone from him'; but writing thus unsteadily, as if art and impulse were at odds, he would mar his pure flame-like diction and the structure of entire poems (excepting *Adonais* and many of the lyrics) with looseness and wastefulness. Arnold thought he had missed his medium and was meant by Nature to write in music.

Bagehot, as his way is, has looked for the root of the matter in the character of the poet's mind, and written more as a student than a judge. The essay is a good example of his theoretic grasp, but the theory, though very illuminative, is too simple to be quite true. The childlike spirit, incapable of an inner conflict, seeing either good or evil, but not the mingled yarn, a lyrist pure and mere— this formula will cover much, but it misses the promise of the greater Shelley whom death prevented, and whose dawning glory Browning so ardently acclaims. For, as Browning thinks, with the new powers glinting in his verse from *Julian and Maddalo* onwards, he might have blended the two great themes—'Power and Love in the absolute' and 'Beauty and Good in the concrete', and thrown 'from his poet's station between both, swifter, subtler, and more numerous films for the connexion of each with each' than any other modern writer. And with the closer grip of reality—so the argument seems to run—the buoyancy in him would have had it out with the heaviness in a philosophy that would have 'ranged him with the Christians'.

So stand the indictment and the defence, and the reader
must take them to his own court. But as the two longer
pieces of criticism chosen for this book are in some contra-
diction, it may not be amiss to set down briefly the intermediate view.

'Ideal Shelley, statue-blind'—Was he, as Bagehot supposes,
this by nature, and this only, or was he inclining effectually
Shakespeare's way, and blending, or about to blend, two
orders of poetry? No doubt, he would have gone on trying
to describe men as they live and move, in dramas like the
unfinished *Charles the First*, or that projected on Tasso, or
perhaps in the long-contemplated poem which should have
been, like *Don Juan*, 'something new, and relative to the
age', and yet beautiful. But the ideality of his moral vision
would be inconvertible. He had no portion at all, as his
satires show, in the sphere of comedy, and a character in his
hands is nothing more definite than a moral temper or spirit
in some ideal figure. Even *The Cenci*, with all its pity and
terror, is a drama of emotion, and not one of character. The
force of these deficiencies would probably have confined
him in the end to the kind of poetry in which his strength
lay, and which, as Swinburne has argued in the pages given
in this book, cannot be measured with any that takes for its
province 'this much-loved earth'. It is the great kind of
Aeschylus, Dante, Calderon, Milton, in all of whom Shelley
was deeply read; a poetry of the contention of spiritual
principles, 'mighty opposites', in the field of time, and the
brunt in the heart of man, and the ardours and sublimities in
man or nature that have in them a touch of the infinite.
For these poets it has always been a hard essay to bring
together the familiar and the sublime, but Shelley might have
brought to it the fine realism of *Julian and Maddalo*, and
mixed that and other acquisitions, perhaps, as has been
suggested, into a drama like Calderon's, or into 'visions' or

'pageants' like *The Triumph of Life*. But, whatever was
probable or possible, we have no need to be drawing cheques
on his 'unfulfilled renown'; for nothing in English verse
stands surer than some of his poetry of 'Power and Love in
the absolute'. It is true there is something strange, as well as
something matchless, in the woof of his lyric poems, and
especially the shortest. The critics complain that the passion
blazes but does not glow, that the lover knows not whom to
love, but wastes his ardour on wind and cloud and metaphysical being. Indeed, he often adverted to his habit of pro-
viding the affections with alternatives or supplements to
humanity, 'connecting himself', as he put it, with 'everything that exists'. He writes in the essay *On Life*:

Let us recollect our sensations as children. What a distinct and
intense apprehension had we of the world and of ourselves! . . .
We less habitually distinguished all that we saw and felt from
ourselves. They seemed as it were to constitute one mass.
There are some persons who, in this respect, are always children.

He is one of these; blending himself with nature, imparting
to her his own rejoicings and wants. And the faith in the
other existence that 'rights the disaster of this', and the one
beauty in its temporal shapes, and 'the fire for which all
things thirst', is conceived and fostered in that intimacy.
When, therefore, he unites in one passion, in 'a mist of
sense and thought', the burdens of his heart and mind, and
seems to utter not more his own desire than the wide
world's, the note is high and rare, and the easy and entire
response can come only from the few who were born to it,
or the many more whom he has educated to enjoy him.
But he could never have stood at all were there no good
wine in the strange cup, were his verse not rooted in
nature and in the eternal need of love. If Shelley holds
his own among the poets, it is because he is not 'ethereal',
but has looked far into a great heart, and 'draws us with the
cords of a man'.

SHELLEY'S LIFE

1792. August 4, Percy Bysshe Shelley born at Field Place, Warnham, near Horsham.

1802–4. At Sion House Academy, near Brentford.

1804 midsummer—1810. At Eton.

1810. Publishes *Zastrozzi* (April), and *Original Poetry by Victor and Cazire* (September). October, enters University College, Oxford, and meets Thomas Jefferson Hogg. Publishes *Posthumous Fragments of Margaret Nicholson* (November), and *St. Irvyne, or the Rosicrucian* (December). Breach with Harriet Grove, Christmas Vacation.

1811. Expelled from University College in consequence of his pamphlet *The Necessity of Atheism*, March 25. Correspondence with Elizabeth Hitchener, June 1811–June 1812. August 28, marries Harriet Westbrook. November, goes to live at Keswick, and meets Southey.

1812. January, opens correspondence with William Godwin. February 12–April 4, visits Ireland; distributes his *Address to the Irish People* and speaks on Catholic Emancipation in Dublin. April, to Nantgwillt, near Rhayader; (?) meets T. L. Peacock for the first time. June–August, at Lynmouth; writes *A Letter to Lord Ellenborough*, and works at *Queen Mab*. August, to Tremadoc, Carnarvon. October, meets Godwin in London.

1813. February, finishes *Queen Mab* (published in the summer); leaves Tremadoc on second visit to Ireland (Killarney, Cork). April, in London. June, birth of his daughter Ianthe. July–October, at Bracknell, Berkshire. October–December, in Edinburgh. December, takes a house in Windsor; in the following months frequently at Bracknell and in London.

1814. Early in the year, publishes *A Refutation of Deism*. July, final breach with Harriet, and union with Mary Wollstonecraft Godwin. July 28–mid-September, France, Switzerland, the Rhine. November, birth of Harriet's second child, Charles Bysshe.

1815. January, in command of a large income on the death of his grandfather, Sir Bysshe Shelley. August, settles at Bishopsgate, near Windsor; autumn, writes *Alastor*.

1816. January, Mary's first child, William born. March, *Alastor* published. May–September, near Geneva; intercourse with Byron. December 10, Harriet's suicide discovered. December 30, marries Mary Godwin. From the close of this year to departure for Italy in touch with Leigh Hunt and his circle.

1817. February 5, first meeting with Keats. March, settles at Great Marlow; deprived of the custody of Harriet's children by the Court of Chancery. Works upon *Prince Athanase* and *Rosalind and Helen*; writes *The Revolt of Islam*, and *A Proposal for putting Reform to the Vote*. September 2, birth of his daughter Clara.

1818. January, *The Revolt of Islam* published. April, arrives in Italy.
    Visits Pisa, Leghorn, the Baths of Lucca. August, at Venice
    with Byron. September, to Este. Death of his daughter
    Clara. Writes *Lines among the Euganean Hills, Julian and
    Maddalo, Prometheus Unbound*, Act I (almost all). Novem-
    ber, visits Rome and Pompeii, and settles in Naples.

1819. February, leaves Naples; *Rosalind and Helen* published
    (spring). March 5–June 10, in Rome; writes *Prometheus
    Unbound*, Acts II and III. June 7, death of his son William.
    June–October, near Leghorn and the Gisbornes; *The Cenci*,
    begun at Rome, is finished. October, to Florence. November,
    birth of his son Percy Florence. Writes *A Philosophical
    View of Reform, The Mask of Anarchy, Peter Bell the Third,
    Ode to the West Wind, Prometheus Unbound*, Act IV.

1820. January, to Pisa. June, to the Gisbornes' house at Leghorn.
    Writes *A Letter to Maria Gisborne. Prometheus Unbound* and
    other poems published (summer). August, to San Giuliano,
    near Pisa. Writes *The Witch of Atlas* and *Oedipus Tyrannus*.
    October 31, returns to Pisa. Begins to gather circle of
    friends: Medwin, Mavrocordato, Emilia Viviani.

1821. January–February, writes *Epipsychidion* (published in the
    summer). February, death of Keats. February–March,
    writes *A Defence of Poetry*; makes friends with Edward and
    Jane Williams. May 8–October 25, mostly at San Giuliano.
    June, writes *Adonais* (printed at Pisa in July). August,
    visits Byron at Ravenna. Writes *Hellas* (autumn). October,
    Byron moves to Pisa.

1822. January, Edward John Trelawny joins the circle at Pisa.
    Hellas published (spring). May 1, moves to Casa Magni, near
    Lerici, on the Bay of Spezzia. June, works on *The Triumph
    of Life*. June 20, meets Leigh Hunt at Leghorn. July 8,
    drowned at sea.

1824. *Posthumous Poems*, ed. Mrs. Shelley.

1833. *The Shelley Papers*, with unpublished poems, ed. Medwin.

1839. *The Poetical Works*, ed. Mrs. Shelley, in four volumes. Second
    edition in one volume.

1840. *Essays, Letters from Abroad, Translations, and Fragments*, ed.
    Mrs. Shelley, in two volumes.

THE following editions have been consulted in the compilation of
the notes: *The Poems of Percy Bysshe Shelley*, edited with notes by
C. D. Locock (Methuen); *Adonais*, edited by W. M. Rossetti, a new
edition revised with the assistance of A. O. Prickard (Oxford University Press); and *Peacock's Four Ages of Poetry, Shelley's Defence of
Poetry, Browning's Essay on Shelley*, edited by H. F. B. Brett-Smith
(Blackwell). Except a very few unimportant changes of punctuation,
the text of the poetry is that of the Oxford Shelley, ed. Thomas
Hutchinson.

ROBERT BROWNING ON SHELLEY

(From Robert Browning's *Essay on Shelley*. Written as an Introduction to the volume of twenty-five spurious *Letters of Shelley*, published by Edward Moxon in 1852)

DOUBTLESS we accept gladly the biography of an objective poet, as the phrase now goes; one whose endeavour has been to reproduce things external (whether the phenomena of the scenic universe, or the manifested action of the human heart and brain) with an immediate reference, in every case, to the common eye and apprehension of his fellow men, assumed capable of receiving and profiting by this reproduction. It has been obtained through the poet's double faculty of seeing external objects more clearly, widely, and deeply, than is possible to the average mind, at the same 10 time that he is so acquainted and in sympathy with its narrower comprehension as to be careful to supply it with no other materials than it can combine into an intelligible whole.

We turn with stronger needs to the genius of an opposite tendency—the subjective poet of modern classification. He, gifted like the objective poet with the fuller perception of nature and man, is impelled to embody the thing he perceives, not so much with reference to the many below as to the one above him, the supreme Intelligence which 20 apprehends all things in their absolute truth—an ultimate view ever aspired to, if but partially attained, by the poet's own soul. Not what man sees, but what God sees—the *Ideas* of Plato, seeds of creation lying burningly on the Divine Hand—it is toward these that he struggles. Not with the combination of humanity in action, but with the primal elements of humanity he has to do; and he digs where he stands—preferring to seek them in his own soul as the nearest reflex of that absolute Mind, according to the

B

intuitions of which he desires to perceive and speak. Such a poet does not deal habitually with the picturesque groupings and tempestuous tossings of the forest-trees, but with their roots and fibres naked to the chalk and stone. He does not paint pictures and hang them on the walls, but rather carries them on the retina of his own eyes: we must look deep into his human eyes, to see those pictures on them. He is rather a seer, accordingly, than a fashioner, and what he produces will be less a work than an effluence.
10 That effluence cannot be easily considered in abstraction from his personality—being indeed the very radiance and aroma of his personality, projected from it but not separated. Therefore, in our approach to the poetry, we necessarily approach the personality of the poet; in apprehending it we apprehend him, and certainly we cannot love it without loving him. But for love's and for understanding's sake we desire to know him, and as readers of his poetry must be readers of his biography also.

I shall observe, in passing, that it seems not so much
20 from any essential distinction in the faculty of the two poets or in the nature of the objects contemplated by either, as in the more immediate adaptability of these objects to the distinct purpose of each, that the objective poet, in his appeal to the aggregate human mind, chooses to deal with the doings of men (the result of which dealing, in its pure form, when even description, as suggesting a describer, is dispensed with, is what we call dramatic poetry), while the subjective poet, whose study has been himself, appealing through himself to the absolute Divine mind, prefers to
30 dwell upon those external scenic appearances which strike out most abundantly and uninterruptedly his inner light and power, selects that silence of the earth and sea in which he can best hear the beating of his individual heart, and leaves the noisy, complex, yet imperfect exhibitions of

nature in the manifold experience of man around him,
which serve only to distract and suppress the working of his
brain. These opposite tendencies of genius will be more
readily descried in their artistic effect than in their moral
spring and cause. Pushed to an extreme and manifested
as a deformity, they will be seen plainest of all in the fault
of either artist, when subsidiarily to the human interest of
his work his occasional illustrations from scenic nature are
introduced as in the earlier works of the originative painters
—men and women filling the foreground with consummate 10
mastery, while mountain, grove and rivulet show like an
anticipatory revenge on that succeeding race of landscape-
painters whose 'figures' disturb the perfection of their earth
and sky. It would be idle to inquire, of these two kinds of
poetic faculty in operation, which is the higher or even
rarer endowment. If the subjective might seem to be the
ultimate requirement of every age, the objective, in the
strictest state, must still retain its original value. For it is
with this world, as starting-point and basis alike, that we
shall always have to concern ourselves: the world is not to be 20
learned and thrown aside, but reverted to and relearned.
The spiritual comprehension may be infinitely subtilised,
but the raw material it operates upon, must remain. There
may be no end of the poets who communicate to us what they
see in an object with reference to their own individuality;
what it was before they saw it, in reference to the aggregate
human mind, will be as desirable to know as ever. Nor is
there any reason why these two modes of poetic faculty
may not issue hereafter from the same poet in successive
perfect works, examples of which, according to what are 30
now considered the exigences of art, we have hitherto
possessed in distinct individuals only. A mere running in
of the one faculty upon the other is, of course, the ordinary
circumstance. Far more rarely it happens that either is

found so decidedly prominent and superior, as to be pronounced comparatively pure: while of the perfect shield, with the gold and silver side set up for all comers to challenge, there has yet been no instance.

A full life of Shelley should be written at once, while the materials for it continue in reach; not to minister to the curiosity of the public, but to obliterate the last stain of that false life which was forced on the public's attention before it had any curiosity on the matter—a biography, composed
10 in harmony with the present general disposition to have faith in him, yet not shrinking from a candid statement of all ambiguous passages, through a reasonable confidence that the most doubtful of them will be found consistent with a belief in the eventual perfection of his character, according to the poor limits of our humanity. Nor will men persist in confounding, any more than God confounds, with genuine infidelity and an atheism of the heart, those passionate, impatient struggles of a boy towards distant truth and love, made in the dark, and ended by one sweep
20 of the natural seas before the full moral sunrise could shine out on him. Crude convictions of boyhood, conveyed in imperfect and inapt forms of speech—for such things all boys have been pardoned. There are growing-pains, accompanied by temporary distortion, of the soul also. And it would be hard indeed upon this young Titan of genius, murmuring in divine music his human ignorances, through his very thirst for knowledge, and his rebellion, in mere aspiration to law, if the melody itself substantiated the error, and the tragic cutting short of life perpetuated into
30 sins such faults as, under happier circumstances, would have been left behind by the consent of the most arrogant moralist, forgotten on the lowest steps of youth.

The responsibility of presenting to the public a biography of Shelley, does not, however, lie with me: I have only to

make it a little easier by arranging these few supplementary
letters, with a recognition of the value of the whole collec-
tion. This value I take to consist in a most truthful con-
formity of the Correspondence, in its limited degree, with
the moral and intellectual character of the writer as displayed
in the highest manifestations of his genius. Letters and
poems are obviously an act of the same mind, produced by
the same law, only differing in the application to the individual or collective understanding. Letters and poems
may be used indifferently as the basement of our opinion 10
upon the writer's character; the finished expression of a
sentiment in the poems giving light and significance to the
rudiments of the same in the letters, and these, again, in
their incipiency and unripeness, authenticating the exalted
mood and reattaching it to the personality of the writer.
The musician speaks on the note he sings with; there is no
change in the scale, as he diminishes the volume into
familiar intercourse. There is nothing of that jarring
between the man and the author which has been found so
amusing or so melancholy; no dropping of the tragic mask, 20
as the crowd melts away; no mean discovery of the real
motives of a life's achievement, often, in other lives, laid
bare as pitifully as when, at the close of a holiday, we catch
sight of the internal lead-pipes and wood-valves to which,
and not to the ostensible conch and dominant Triton of the
fountain, we have owed our admired waterwork. No breaking out, in household privacy, of hatred anger and scorn,
incongruous with the higher mood and suppressed artisti-
cally in the book: no brutal return to self-delighting, when
the audience of philanthropic schemes is out of hearing: no 30
indecent stripping off the grander feeling and rule of life
as too costly and cumbrous for every-day wear. Whatever
Shelley was, he was with an admirable sincerity. It was not
always truth that he thought and spoke; but in the purity

of truth he spoke and thought always. Everywhere is apparent his belief in the existence of Good, to which Evil is an accident; his faithful holding by what he assumed to be the former, going everywhere in company with the tenderest pity for those acting or suffering on the opposite hypothesis. For he was tender, though tenderness is not always the characteristic of very sincere natures; he was eminently both tender and sincere. And not only do the same affection and yearning after the well-being of his kind

10 appear in the letters as in the poems, but they express themselves by the same theories and plans, however crude and unsound. There is no reservation of a subtler, less costly, more serviceable remedy for his own ill than he has proposed for the general one; nor does he ever contemplate an object on his own account from a less elevation than he uses in exhibiting it to the world. How shall we help believing Shelley to have been, in his ultimate attainment, the splendid spirit of his own best poetry, when we find even his carnal speech to agree faithfully, at faintest as at

20 strongest, with the tone and rhythm of his most oracular utterances?

I conjecture, from a review of the various publications of Shelley's youth, that one of the causes of his failure at the outset was the peculiar *practicalness* of his mind, which was not without a determinate effect on his progress in theorizing. An ordinary youth, who turns his attention to similar subjects, discovers falsities, incongruities, and various points for amendment, and, in the natural advance of the purely critical spirit unchecked by considerations of remedy,

30 keeps up before his young eyes so many instances of the same error and wrong that he finds himself unawares arrived at the startling conclusion, that all must be changed —or nothing: in the face of which plainly impossible achievement he is apt (looking perhaps a little more serious

by the time he touches at the decisive issue) to feel, either carelessly or considerately, that his own attempting a single piece of service would be worse than useless even, and to refer the whole task to another age and person—safe in proportion to his incapacity. Wanting words to speak, he has never made a fool of himself by speaking. But, in Shelley's case, the early fervour and power to *see* was accompanied by as precocious a fertility to *contrive*: he endeavoured to realize as he went on idealizing; every wrong had simultaneously its remedy, and, out of the strength of his hatred for the former, he took the strength of his confidence in the latter—till suddenly he stood pledged to the defence of a set of miserable little expedients, just as if they represented great principles, and to an attack upon various great principles, really so, without leaving himself time to examine whether, because they were antagonistical to the remedy he had suggested, they must therefore be identical or even essentially connected with the wrong he sought to cure—playing with blind passion into the hands of his enemies, and dashing at whatever red cloak was held forth to him, as the cause of the fireball he had last been stung with—mistaking Churchdom for Christianity, and for marriage 'the sale of love' and the law of sexual oppression.

Gradually, however, he was leaving behind him this low practical dexterity, unable to keep up with his widening intellectual perception; and, in exact proportion as he did so, his true power strengthened and proved itself. Gradually he was raised above the contemplation of spots and the attempt at effacing them to the great Abstract Light, and through the discrepancy of the creation to the sufficiency of the First Cause. Gradually he was learning that the best way of removing abuses is to stand fast by truth. Truth is one, as they are manifold; and innumerable negative effects

are produced by the upholding of one positive principle.
I shall say what I think—had Shelley lived he would have
finally ranged himself with the Christians; his very instinct
for helping the weaker side (if numbers make strength), his
very 'hate of hate', which at first mistranslated itself into
delirious *Queen Mab* notes and the like, would have got
clearer-sighted by exercise. The preliminary step to following Christ is the leaving the dead to bury their dead—not
clamouring on His doctrine for an especial solution of
10 difficulties which are referable to the general problem of the
universe. Already he had attained to a profession of 'a
worship to the Spirit of good within, which requires (before
it sends that inspiration forth, which impresses its likeness
upon all it creates) devoted and disinterested homage', as
Coleridge says—and Paul likewise. And we find in one of his
last exquisite fragments, avowedly a record of one of his own
mornings and its experience, as it dawned on him at his soul
and body's best in his boat on the Serchio—that as surely as

> The stars burnt out in the pale blue air,
20 > And the thin white moon lay withering there—
> Day had kindled the dewy woods,
> And the rocks above, and the stream below,
> And the vapours in their multitudes,
> And the Apennine's shroud of summer snow—
> Day had awakened all things that be;

just so surely, he tells us (stepping forward from this
delicious dance-music, choragus-like, into the grander
measure befitting the final enunciation),

> All rose to do the task He set to each,
30 > Who shaped us to His ends and not our own;
> The million rose to learn, and One to teach
> What none yet ever knew or can be known.

No more difference than this, from David's pregnant
conclusion so long ago!

Meantime, as I call Shelley a moral man, because he was
true, simple-hearted, and brave, and because what he acted

corresponded to what he knew, so I call him a man of religious mind, because every audacious negative cast up by him against the Divine was interpenetrated with a mood of reverence and adoration—and because I find him everywhere taking for granted some of the capital dogmas of Christianity, while most vehemently denying their historical basement. There is such a thing as an efficacious knowledge of and belief in the politics of Junius or the poetry of Rowley, though a man should at the same time dispute the title of Chatterton to the one, and consider the author of the other, as Byron wittily did, 'really, truly, no-body at all.'[1] There is even such a thing, we come to learn wonderingly in these very letters, as a profound sensibility and adaptitude for art, while the science of the percipient is so little advanced as to admit of his stronger admiration for Guido (and Carlo Dolce!) than for Michael Angelo. A Divine Being has Himself said, that 'a word against the Son of man shall be forgiven to a man', while 'a word against the Spirit of God' (implying a general deliberate preference of perceived evil to perceived good) 'shall not be forgiven to a man'. Also, in religion, one earnest and unextorted assertion of belief should outweigh, as a matter of testimony, many assertions of unbelief. The fact that there is a gold-region is established by the finding of one lump, though you miss the vein never so often.

[1] Or, to take our illustrations from the writings of Shelley himself, there is such a thing as admirably appreciating a work by Andrea Verocchio—and fancifully characterizing the Pisan Torre Guelfa by the Ponte a Mare, black against the sunsets—and consummately painting the islet of San Clemente with its penitentiary for rebellious priests, to the west between Venice and the Lido—while you believe the first to be a fragment of an antique sarcophagus—the second, Ugolino's Tower of Famine (the vestiges of which should be sought for in the Piazza de' Cavalieri)—and the third (as I convinced myself last summer at Venice), San Servolo with its madhouse—which, far from being 'windowless', is as full of windows as a barrack.

He died before his youth ended. In taking the measure of him as a man, he must be considered on the whole and at his ultimate spiritual stature, and not be judged of at the immaturity and by the mistakes of ten years before: that, indeed, would be to judge of the author of *Julian and Maddalo* by *Zastrozzi*. Let the whole truth be told of his worst mistake. I believe, for my own part, that if anything could now shame or grieve Shelley, it would be an attempt to vindicate him at the expense of another.

10   Let me conclude with a thought of Shelley as a poet. In the hierarchy of creative minds, it is the presence of the highest faculty that gives first rank, in virtue of its kind, not degree; no pretension of a lower nature, whatever the completeness of development or variety of effect, impeding the precedency of the rarer endowment though only in the germ. The contrary is sometimes maintained; it is attempted to make the lower gifts (which are potentially included in the higher faculty) of independent value, and equal to some exercise of the special function. For instance,
20 should not a poet possess common sense? Then the possession of abundant common sense implies a step towards becoming a poet. Yes; such a step as the lapidary's, when, strong in the fact of carbon entering largely into the composition of the diamond, he heaps up a sack of charcoal in order to compete with the Koh-i-noor. I pass at once, therefore, from Shelley's minor excellences to his noblest and predominating characteristic.

This I call his simultaneous perception of Power and Love in the absolute, and of Beauty and Good in the
30 concrete, while he throws, from his poet's station between both, swifter, subtler, and more numerous films for the connexion of each with each, than have been thrown by any modern artificer of whom I have knowledge; proving how, as he says,

The spirit of the worm within the sod,
In love and worship blends itself with God.

I would rather consider Shelley's poetry as a sublime fragmentary essay towards a presentment of the correspondency of the universe to Deity, of the natural to the spiritual, and of the actual to the ideal, than I would isolate and separately appraise the worth of many detachable portions which might be acknowledged as utterly perfect in a lower moral point of view, under the mere conditions of art. It would be easy to take my stand on successful instances of objectivity in Shelley: there is the unrivalled *Cenci*; there is the *Julian and Maddalo* too; there is the magnificent *Ode to Naples*: why not regard, it may be said, the less organized matter as the radiant elemental foam and solution out of which would have been evolved, eventually, creations as perfect even as those? But I prefer to look for the highest attainment, not simply the high—and, seeing it, I hold by it. There is surely enough of the work 'Shelley' to be known enduringly among men, and, I believe, to be accepted of God, as human work may; and around the imperfect proportions of such the most elaborated productions of ordinary art must arrange themselves as inferior illustrations.

It is because I have long held these opinions in assurance and gratitude that I catch at the opportunity offered to me of expressing them here; knowing that the alacrity to fulfil an humble office conveys more love than the acceptance of the honour of a higher one, and that better, therefore, than the signal service it was the dream of my boyhood to render to his fame and memory may be the saying of a few inadequate words upon these scarcely more important supplementary letters of SHELLEY.

PARIS, *Dec. 4th,* 1851.

VERSES BY ROBERT BROWNING

(From *Pauline*. Published 1833)

SUN-TREADER—life and light be thine for ever!
Thou art gone from us—years go by, and spring
Gladdens, and the young earth is beautiful,
Yet thy songs come not—other bards arise,
But none like thee;—they stand—thy majesties,   5
Like mighty works which tell some Spirit there
Hath sat regardless of neglect and scorn,
Till, its long task completed, it hath risen
And left us, never to return: and all
Rush in to peer and praise when all in vain.   10
The air seems bright with thy past presence yet, . . .

WALTER BAGEHOT ON SHELLEY

(From Walter Bagehot's *Essay on Shelley*. First published in *The National Review*, 1856, and reprinted in *Estimates of Some Englishmen and Scotchmen*, 1858)

SHELLEY'S is probably the most remarkable instance of
the pure impulsive character. Some men are born under the
law: their whole life is a continued struggle between the
lower principles of their nature and the higher. These are
what are called men of principle; each of their best actions is
a distinct choice between conflicting motives. In extreme
contrast to this is the nature which has no struggle. It is
possible to conceive a character in which but one impulse is
ever felt—in which the whole being, as with a single breeze,
10 is carried in a single direction. Of course this may be a
quality of the highest character: indeed, in the highest
character it will certainly be found; no one will question that
the whole nature of the holiest being tends to what is holy
without let, struggle, or strife—it would be impiety to

doubt it. Completely realized on earth this idea will never be; but approximations may be found, and one of the closest of those approximations is Shelley. We fancy his mind placed in the light of thought, with pure subtle fancies playing to and fro. On a sudden an impulse arises; it is alone, and has nothing to contend with; it cramps the intellect, pushes aside the fancies, constrains the nature: it *bolts* forward into action. Such a character is an extreme puzzle to external observers. From the occasionality of its impulses it will often seem silly; from their singularity, strange; from their intensity, fanatical. It is absurdest in the more trifling matters. There is a legend of Shelley, during an early visit to London, flying along the street, catching sight of a new microscope, buying it in a moment; pawning it the instant afterwards to relieve some one in the same street in distress. The trait may be exaggerated, but it is characteristic. It shows the sudden irruption of his impulses, their abrupt force and curious purity.

The predominant impulse in Shelley from a very early age was 'a passion for reforming mankind.' The impulse was upon him. He would have been ready to preach that mankind were to be 'free, equal, pure, and wise', in the Ottoman empire, or to the Czar, or to George III. Such truths were independent of time and place and circumstance; some time or other, something or somebody would most certainly intervene to establish them. It was this placid undoubting confidence which irritated the positive and sceptical mind of Hazlitt. 'The author of the *Prometheus Unbound*', he tells us, 'has a fire in his eye, a fever in his blood, a maggot in his brain, a hectic flutter in his speech, which mark out the philosophic fanatic. He is sanguine-complexioned and shrill-voiced. As is often observable in the case of religious enthusiasts, there is a slenderness of constitutional stamina, which renders the flesh no match for the spirit. His bending

flexible form appears to take no strong hold of things, does
not grapple with the world about him, but slides from it like
a river.   The shock of accident, the weight of authority,
make no impression on his opinions, which retire like a
feather, or rise from the encounter unhurt, through their
own buoyancy. He is clogged by no dull system of reali-
ties, no earth-bound feelings, no rooted prejudices, by
nothing that belongs to the mighty trunk and hard
husk of nature and habit; but is drawn up by irresistible
10 levity to the regions of mere speculation and fancy, to the
sphere of air and fire, where his delighted spirit floats in
' seas of pearl and clouds of amber'.

Another passion, which no man has ever felt more strongly
than Shelley—the desire to penetrate the mysteries of existence (by Hazlitt profanely called curiosity)—is depicted in
Alastor as the sole passion of the only person in the poem.
He is cheered on his way by a beautiful dream, and the
search to find it again mingles with the shadowy quest.
It is remarkable how great is the superiority of the personi-
20 fication in *Alastor*, though one of his earliest writings, over
the reforming abstractions of his other works. The reason is,
its far greater closeness to reality. The one is a description
of what he was; the other of what he desired to be. Shelley
had nothing of the magic influence, the large insight, the
bold strength, the permeating eloquence which fit a man for
a practical reformer; but he had, in perhaps an unequalled
and unfortunate measure, the famine of the intellect—the
daily insatiable craving after the highest truth—which is the
passion of *Alastor*.

30   We have shown that no character except his own, and
characters most strictly allied to his own, are delineated in
his works. The tendency of his mind was rather to personify
isolated qualities or impulses—equality, liberty, revenge,
and so on—than to create out of separate parts or passions

the single conception of an entire character. This is, properly speaking, the mythological tendency. All early
nations show this marked disposition to conceive of separate
forces and qualities as a kind of semi-persons; that is, not
true actual persons with distinct characters, but beings who
guide certain influences, and of whom all we know is that
they guide those influences. Shelley evinces a remarkable
tendency to deal with mythology in this simple and elementary form. Other poets have breathed into mythology a
modern life; have been attracted by those parts which seem 10
to have a religious meaning, and have enlarged that meaning
while studying to embody it. With Shelley it is otherwise;
the parts of mythology by which he is attracted are the bare
parts—the simple stories which Dr. Johnson found so
tedious. When not writing on topics connected with ancient
mythology, Shelley shows the same bent. *The Cloud* and
the *Skylark* are more like mythology—have more of the
impulse by which the populace, if we may so say, of the
external world was first fancied into existence—than any
other modern poems. There is, indeed, no habit of mind 20
more remote from our solid and matter-of-fact existence;
none which was once powerful, of which the present traces
are so rare.

The works of Shelley lie in a confused state, like the *dis-*
jecta membra of the poet of our boyhood. They are in the
strictest sense 'remains'. It is absurd to expect from a man
who died at thirty a long work of perfected excellence. All
which at so early an age can be expected are fine fragments,
casual expressions of single inspirations. Of these Shelley
has written some that are nearly, and one or two perhaps 30
that are quite, perfect. But he has not done more. It would
have been better if he had not attempted so much. He
would have done well to have heeded Goethe's caution to
Eckermann: 'Beware of attempting a large work. If you

have a great work in your head, nothing else thrives near it, all other thoughts are repelled, and the pleasantness of life itself is for the time lost. What exertion and expenditure of mental force are required to arrange and round off a great whole; and then what powers, and what a tranquil undisturbed situation in life, to express it with the proper fluency! If you have erred as to the whole, all your toil is lost; and further, if, in treating so extensive a subject, you are not perfectly master of your material in the details, the whole
10 will be defective, and censure will be incurred.' Shelley did not know this. He was ever labouring at long poems: but he has left scarcely one which, as a whole, is worthy of him; you can point to none and say, This is Shelley. Even had he lived to an age of riper capacity, it may be doubted if a being so discontinuous, so easily hurried to and fro, would have possessed the settled, undeviating self-devotion that are necessary to a long and perfect composition. He had not, like Goethe, the cool shrewdness to watch for inspiration.

His success, as we have said, is in fragments; and the best
20 of those fragments are lyrical. The very same isolation and suddenness of impulse which rendered him unfit for the composition of great works rendered him peculiarly fit to pour forth on a sudden the intense essence of peculiar feeling 'in profuse strains of unpremeditated art'. Mr. Macaulay has said that the words 'bard' and 'inspiration', generally so meaningless when applied to modern poets, have a meaning when applied to Shelley. An idea, an emotion grew upon his brain; his breast heaved, his frame shook, his nerves quivered with the 'harmonious madness' of imaginative
30 concentration. 'Poetry', he himself tells us, 'is not, like reasoning, a power to be exerted according to the determination of the will. A man cannot say, "I will compose poetry." The greatest poet even cannot say it; for the mind in creation is as a fading coal, which some invisible influence, like an

inconstant wind, awakens to transitory brightness; this power arises from within, like the colour of a flower which fades and changes as it is developed, and the conscious portions of our natures are unprophetic either of its approach or its departure.'

In most poets unearthly beings are introduced to express peculiar removed essences of lyrical rapture; but they are generally failures. Lord Byron tried this kind of composition in *Manfred*, and the result is an evident failure. In Shelley, such singing solitary beings are almost uniformly successful; while writing, his mind really for the moment was in the state in which theirs is supposed always to be. He loved attenuated ideas and abstracted excitement. In expressing their nature he had but to set free his own. Human nature is not, however, long equal to this sustained effort of remote excitement. The impulse fails, imagination fades, inspiration dies away. . . . 'The world', says Mr. Emerson, 'is mundane.' A creeping sense of weight is part of the most aspiring nature. To the most thrilling rapture succeeds despondency, perhaps pain. To Shelley this was peculiarly natural. His dreams of reform, of a world which was to be, called up the imaginative ecstasy: his soul bounded forward into the future; but it is not possible even to the most abstracted and excited mind to place its happiness in the expected realisation of impossible schemes, and yet not occasionally be uncertain of those schemes. . . . No man can always dream of ever altering all which is. It is characteristic of Shelley, that at the end of his most rapturous and sanguine lyrics there intrudes the cold consciousness of this world. In many of his poems the failing of the feeling is as beautiful as its short moment of hope and buoyancy.

When we attempt to distinguish the imagination from the fancy, we find that they are often related as a beginning to an ending. On a sudden, we do not know how, a new image, form, idea, occurs to our minds; sometimes it is borne in upon us with a flash, sometimes we seem unawares to stumble upon it, and find it as if it had long been there: in either case the involuntary unanticipated appearance of this new thought or image is a primitive fact which we cannot analyse or account for. We say it originated in our imagination or creative faculty: but this is a mere expression of the completeness of our ignorance; we could only define the imagination as the faculty which produces such effects; we know nothing of it or its constitution. Again, on this original idea a large number of accessory and auxiliary ideas seem to grow or accumulate insensibly, casually, and without our intentional effort; the bare primitive form attracts a clothing of delicate materials—an adornment not altering its essence, but enhancing its effect. This we call the work of the fancy. An exquisite delicacy in appropriating fitting accessories is as much the characteristic excellence of a fanciful mind, as the possession of large, simple, bold ideas is of an imaginative one.   There is something statuesque about the imagination; there is the gradual complexity of painting in the most exquisite productions of the fancy. When we speak of this distinction, we seem almost to be speaking of the distinction between ancient and modern literature.   The characteristic of the classical literature is the simplicity with which the imagination appears in it; that of modern literature is the profusion with which the most various adornments of the accessory fancy are thrown and lavished upon it.

It is only necessary to open Shelley to show how essentially classical in its highest efforts his art is. Indeed, although nothing can be further removed from the staple topics of the classical writers than the abstract lyric, yet their treatment is nearly essential to it. We have said, its sphere is in what the Germans call the unconditioned—in

the unknown, immeasurable, and untrodden. It follows
from this that we cannot know much about it. We cannot
know detail in tracts we have never visited; the infinite has
no form; the immeasurable no outline: that which is common
to all worlds is simple. There is therefore no scope for the
accessory fancy. With a single soaring effort imagination
may reach her end: if she fail, no fancy can help her; if she
succeed, there will be no petty accumulations of insensible
circumstance in a region far above all things. Shelley's
excellence in the abstract lyric is almost another phrase for 10
the simplicity of his impulsive imagination. He shows it on
other subjects also. We have spoken of his bare treatment
of the ancient mythology. It is the same with his treatment
of nature. In the description of the celestial regions the
details are few, the air thin, the lights distinct. We are conscious of an essential difference if we compare the *Ode to
the Nightingale* in Keats with the *Ode to a Skylark*. We
can hear that the poetry of Keats is a rich, composite,
voluptuous harmony; that of Shelley a clear single ring of
penetrating melody.   20

The sensibility of Keats was attracted too by the spectacle
of the universe; he could not keep his eye from seeing, or his
ears from hearing, the glories of it. All the beautiful objects
of nature reappear by name in his poetry. The abstract
idea of beauty is for ever celebrated in Shelley; it haunted
his soul. But it was independent of special things; it was
the general surface of beauty which lies upon all things. It
was the smile of the universe and the expression of the world;
it was not the vision of a land of corn and wine.

In style, said Mr. Wordsworth—in workmanship, we think 30
his expression was—Shelley is one of the best of us. This
too, we think, was the second of the peculiarities to which
Mr. Macaulay referred when he said that Shelley had, more
than any recent poet, some of the qualities of the great old

masters. The peculiarity of his style is its intellectuality;
and this strikes us the more from its contrast with his im-
pulsiveness. He had something of this in life. Hurried
away by sudden desires as he was in his choice of ends, we are
struck with a certain comparative measure and adjustment
in his choice of means. So in his writings: over the most
intense excitement, the grandest objects, the keenest agony,
the most buoyant joy, he throws an air of subtle mind. His
language is minutely and acutely searching; at the dizziest
10 height of meaning the keenness of the words is greatest.
It was from Plato and Sophocles, doubtless, that he gained
the last perfection in preserving the accuracy of the intellect
when treating of the objects of the imagination; but in its
essence it was a peculiarity of his own nature.

SWINBURNE ON TEXT OF SHELLEY

(From Swinburne's *Notes on the Text of Shelley*. First published in
The Fortnightly Review, May 1869, and included in *Essays and
Studies*, 1875)

MR. ARNOLD, with whose clear and critical spirit it is
always good to come in contact, as disciple or as dissenter,
has twice spoken of Shelley, each time, as I think, putting
forth a brilliant error, shot through and spotted with
glimpses of truth. Byron and Shelley, he says, 'two members of the aristocratic class', alone in their day, strove 'to
apply the modern spirit' to English literature. 'Aristocracies
are, as such, naturally impenetrable by ideas; but their individual members have a high courage and a turn for
10 breaking bounds; and a man of genius, who is the born
child of the idea, happening to be born in the aristocratic
ranks, chafes against the obstacles which prevent him from
freely developing it.' To the truth of this he might have
cited a third witness; for of the English poets then living,

three only were children of the social or political idea, strong
enough to breathe and work in the air of revolution, to
wrestle with change and hold fast the new liberty, to believe
at all in the godhead of people or peoples, in the absolute
right and want of the world, equality of justice, of work and
truth and life; and these three came all out of the same
rank, were all born into one social sect, men of historic
blood and name, having nothing to ask of revolution, nothing
(as the phrase is now) to gain by freedom, but leave to love
and serve the light for the light's sake. Landor, who died 10
last, was eldest, and Shelley, who died first, was youngest of
the three. Each stood alike apart from the rest, far unlike
as each was to the other two; not, like Coleridge, blind to the
things of the time, nor, like Keats, practically alien to all
things but art; and leaving to Southey or Wordsworth the
official laurels and loyalties of courtly content and satisfied
compliance. Out of their rank the Georges could raise no
recruits to beat the drum of prose or blow the bagpipes of
verse in any royal and constitutional procession towards
nuptial or funereal goal.   20

So far we must go with Mr. Arnold; but I cannot follow
him when he adds that Byron and Shelley failed in their
attempt; that the best 'literary creation' of their time, work
'far more solid and complete than theirs', was due to men
in whom the new spirit was dead or was unborn; that,
therefore, 'their names will be greater than their writings'.
First, I protest against the bracketing of the two names.
With all reserve of reverence for the noble genius and
memory of Byron, I can no more accept him as a poet equal
or even akin to Shelley on any side but one, than I could 30
imagine Shelley endowed with the various, fearless, keen-
eyed, and triumphant energy which makes the greatest of
Byron's works so great. With all his glory of ardour and
vigour and humour, Byron was a singer who could not sing;

Shelley outsang all poets on record but some two or three throughout all time; his depths and heights of inner and outer music are as divine as nature's, and not sooner exhaustible. He was alone the perfect singing-god; his thoughts, words, deeds, all sang together. This between two singing-men is a distinction of some significance; and must be, until the inarticulate poets and their articulate outriders have put down singing-men altogether as unrealities, inexpedient if not afflictive in the commonwealth of
10 M. Proudhon and Mr. Carlyle. Till the dawn of that 'most desired hour, more loved and lovely than all its sisters', these unblessed generations will continue to note the difference, and take some account of it. Again, though in some sense a 'child of the idea', Byron is but a foundling or bastard child; Shelley is born heir, and has it by birthright; to Byron it is a charitable nurse, to Shelley a natural mother. All the more praise, it may be said, to Byron for having seen so much as he did and served so loyally. Be it so then; but let not his imperfect and intermittent service, noble and
20 helpful now, and now alloyed with baser temper or broken short through sloth or spite or habit, be set beside the flawless work and perfect service of Shelley. His whole heart and mind, his whole soul and strength, Byron could not give to the idea at all; neither to art, nor freedom, nor any faith whatever. His life's work therefore falls as short of the standard of Shelley's as of Goethe's work. To compare *Cain* with *Prometheus*, the *Prophecy of Dante* with the *Ode to Naples*, is to compare *Manfred* with *Faust*. Shelley was born a son and soldier of light, an
30 archangel winged and weaponed for angel's work. Byron, with a noble admixture of brighter and purer blood, had in him a cross of the true Philistine breed.

Mr. Arnold, in my view, misconceives and misjudges him not less when set against Keats than when bracketed with

Byron. Keats has indeed a divine magic of language applied to nature; here he is unapproachable; this is his throne, and he may bid all kings of song come bow to it. But his ground is not Shelley's ground; they do not run in the same race at all. The *Ode to Autumn*, among other such poems of Keats, renders nature as no man but Keats ever could. Such poems as the *Lines written among the Euganean Hills* cannot compete with it. But do they compete with it? The poem of Keats, Mr. Arnold says, '*renders* Nature'; the poem of Shelley '*tries to render* her'. It is this that I deny. What Shelley tries to do he does; and he does not try to do the same thing as Keats. The comparison is as empty and profitless as one between the sonnets of Shakespeare and the sonnets of Milton. Shelley never in his life wrote a poem of that exquisite contraction and completeness, within that round and perfect limit. This poem of the Euganean Hills is no piece of spiritual sculpture or painting after the life of natural things. I do not pretend to assign it a higher or a lower place; I say simply that its place is not the same. It is a rhapsody of thought and feeling coloured by contact with nature, but not born of the contact; and such as it is all Shelley's work is, even when most vague and vast in its elemental scope of labour and of aim. A soul as great as the world lays hold on the things of the world; on all life of plants, and beasts, and men; on all likeness of time, and death, and good things and evil. His aim is rather to render the effect of a thing than a thing itself; the soul and spirit of life rather than the living form, the growth rather than the thing grown. And herein he too is unapproachable.

THOMAS J. HOGG ON SHELLEY

(From Thomas Jefferson Hogg's *Life of Shelley*, 1858. First written for *The New Monthly Magazine*, 1832)

[On first meeting Shelley at University College, Oxford, in October 1810] I had leisure to examine, and I may add, to admire, the appearance of my very extraordinary guest. It was a sum of many contradictions. His figure was slight and fragile, and yet his bones and joints were large and strong. He was tall, but he stooped so much, that he seemed of a low stature. His clothes were expensive, and made according to the most approved mode of the day; but they were tumbled, rumpled, unbrushed. His gestures were
10 abrupt, and sometimes violent, occasionally even awkward, yet more frequently gentle and graceful. His complexion was delicate, and almost feminine, of the purest red and white; yet he was tanned and freckled by exposure to the sun, having passed the autumn, as he said, in shooting. His features, his whole face, and particularly his head, were, in fact, unusually small; yet the last *appeared* of a remarkable bulk, for his hair was long and bushy, and in fits of absence, and in the agonies (if I may use the word) of anxious thought, he often rubbed it fiercely with his hands,
20 or passed his fingers quickly through his locks unconsciously, so that it was singularly wild and rough. In times when it was the mode to imitate stage-coachmen as closely as possible in costume, and when the hair was invariably cropped, like that of our soldiers, this eccentricity was very striking. His features were not symmetrical (the mouth, perhaps, excepted), yet was the effect of the whole extremely powerful. They breathed an animation, a fire, an enthusiasm, a vivid and preternatural intelligence, that I never met with in any other countenance. Nor was the moral expression
30 less beautiful than the intellectual; for there was a softness,

a delicacy, a gentleness, and especially (though this will surprise many) that air of profound religious veneration, that characterises the best works, and chiefly the frescoes (and into these they infused their whole souls), of the great masters of Florence and of Rome. I recognised the very peculiar expression in these wonderful productions long afterwards, and with a satisfaction mingled with much sorrow, for it was after the decease of him in whose countenance I had first observed it.

THOMAS LOVE PEACOCK ON SHELLEY

(From Thomas Love Peacock's *Memoirs of Shelley*, Part I.
First printed in *Fraser's Magazine*, June 1858)

HE had a prejudice against theatres which I took some pains to overcome. I induced him one evening to accompany me to a representation of the *School for Scandal*. When, after the scenes which exhibited Charles Surface in his jollity, the scene returned, in the fourth act, to Joseph's library, Shelley said to me—'I see the purpose of this comedy. It is to associate virtue with bottles and glasses, and villainy with books.' I had great difficulty to make him stay to the end. He often talked of 'the withering and perverting spirit of comedy'. I do not think he ever went 10 to another.

TRELAWNY ON SHELLEY

(From Edward John Trelawny's *Records of Shelley, Byron, and the Author*. First published 1858; republished and enlarged 1878)

1. *First Impressions.*

THE Williams's received me in their earnest cordial manner; we had a great deal to communicate to each other, and were in loud and animated conversation, when I was rather put out by observing in the passage near the open door, opposite to where I sat, a pair of glittering eyes steadily fixed on mine; it was too dark to make out whom they belonged to. With the acuteness of a woman, Mrs. Williams's eyes followed the direction of mine, and going to the doorway, she laughingly said,

10 'Come in, Shelley, it's only our friend Tre just arrived.'

Swiftly gliding in, blushing like a girl, a tall thin stripling held out both his hands; and although I could hardly believe as I looked at his flushed, feminine, and artless face that it could be the Poet, I returned his warm pressure. After the ordinary greetings and courtesies he sat down and listened. I was silent from astonishment: was it possible this mild-looking, beardless boy, could be at war with all the world?

Mrs. Williams saw my embarrassment, and to relieve me 20 asked Shelley what book he had in his hand? His face brightened, and he answered briskly.

'Calderon's *Magico Prodigioso*. I am translating some passages in it.'

'Oh, read it to us!'

Shoved off from the shore of common-place incidents that could not interest him, and fairly launched on a theme that did, he instantly became oblivious of everything but the book in his hand. The masterly manner in which he

analysed the genius of the author, his lucid interpretation
of the story, and the ease with which he translated into our
language the most subtle and imaginative passages of the
Spanish poet, were marvellous, as was his command of the
two languages. After this touch of his quality I no longer
doubted his identity; a dead silence ensued; looking up,
I asked,

'Where is he?'

Mrs. Williams said, 'Who? Shelley? Oh, he comes and
goes like a spirit, no one knows when or where.'   10

2. *Fine Frenzy.*

WITH no landmarks to guide me, nor sky to be seen above,
I was bewildered in this wilderness of pines and ponds; so
I sat down, struck a light, and smoked a cigar. A red man
would have known his course by the trees themselves, their
growth, form, and colour; or if a footstep had passed that
day, he would have hit upon its trail. As I mused upon his
sagacity and my own stupidity, the braying of a brother
jackass startled me. He was followed by an old man
picking up pine cones. I asked him if he had seen a stranger?

'L'Inglese malincolico haunts the wood maledetta. I will   20
show you his nest.'

As we advanced, the ground swelled into mounds and
hollows. By-and-by the old fellow pointed with his stick
to a hat, books, and loose papers lying about, and then to
a deep pool of dark glimmering water, saying 'Eccolo!'
I thought he meant that Shelley was in or under the water.
The careless, not to say impatient, way in which the Poet
bore his burden of life, caused a vague dread amongst his
family and friends that he might lose or cast it away at any
moment. The strong light streamed through the opening   30
of the trees. One of the pines, undermined by the water,
had fallen into it. Under its lee, and nearly hidden, sat the

Poet, gazing on the dark mirror beneath, so lost in his bardish reverie that he did not hear my approach. . . .

The day I found Shelley in the pine forest he was writing verses on a guitar. I picked up a fragment, but could only make out the first two lines:

> Ariel, to Miranda take
> This slave of music.

It was a frightful scrawl; words smeared out with his finger, and one upon the other, over and over in tiers, and all run together in most 'admired disorder'; it might have been taken for a sketch of a marsh overgrown with bulrushes, and the blots for wild ducks; such a dashed off daub as self-conceited artists mistake for a manifestation of genius. On my observing this to him, he answered,

'When my brain gets heated with thought, it soon boils, and throws off images and words faster than I can skim them off. In the morning, when cooled down, out of the rude sketch as you justly call it, I shall attempt a drawing.'

Selections from

PERCY BYSSHE SHELLEY

From *Alastor, or The Spirit of Solitude*

(Composed at Bishopsgate Heath, near Windsor Park,
autumn 1815; published March 1816)

Nondum amabam, et amare amabam, quaerebam quid
amarem, amans amare.—*Confess. St. August.*

(i) *The Poet* (ll. 1–128)

EARTH, ocean, air, belovéd brotherhood!
If our great Mother has imbued my soul
With aught of natural piety to feel
Your love, and recompense the boon with mine;
If dewy morn, and odorous noon, and even,   5
With sunset and its gorgeous ministers,
And solemn midnight's tingling silentness;
If autumn's hollow sighs in the sere wood,
And winter robing with pure snow and crowns
Of starry ice the grey grass and bare boughs;   10
If spring's voluptuous pantings when she breathes
Her first sweet kisses, have been dear to me;
If no bright bird, insect, or gentle beast
I consciously have injured, but still loved
And cherished these my kindred; then forgive   15
This boast, belovéd brethren, and withdraw
No portion of your wonted favour now!

Mother of this unfathomable world!
Favour my solemn song, for I have loved
Thee ever, and thee only; I have watched   20
Thy shadow, and the darkness of thy steps,
And my heart ever gazes on the depth
Of thy deep mysteries. I have made my bed

In charnels and on coffins, where black death
Keeps record of the trophies won from thee,   25
Hoping to still these obstinate questionings
Of thee and thine, by forcing some lone ghost
Thy messenger, to render up the tale
Of what we are. In lone and silent hours,
When night makes a weird sound of its own stillness,
Like an inspired and desperate alchymist   31
Staking his very life on some dark hope,
Have I mixed awful talk and asking looks
With my most innocent love, until strange tears
Uniting with those breathless kisses, made   35
Such magic as compels the charmèd night
To render up thy charge: . . . and, though ne'er yet
Thou hast unveiled thy inmost sanctuary,
Enough from incommunicable dream,
And twilight phantasms, and deep noon-day thought, 40
Has shone within me, that serenely now
And moveless, as a long-forgotten lyre
Suspended in the solitary dome
Of some mysterious and deserted fane,
I wait thy breath, Great Parent, that my strain   45
May modulate with murmurs of the air,
And motions of the forests and the sea,
And voice of living beings, and woven hymns
Of night and day, and the deep heart of man.

There was a Poet whose untimely tomb   50
No human hands with pious reverence reared,
But the charmed eddies of autumnal winds
Built o'er his mouldering bones a pyramid
Of mouldering leaves in the waste wilderness:—
A lovely youth,—no mourning maiden decked   55

With weeping flowers, or votive cypress wreath,
The lone couch of his everlasting sleep:—
Gentle, and brave, and generous,—no lorn bard
Breathed o'er his dark fate one melodious sigh:
He lived, he died, he sung, in solitude.   60
Strangers have wept to hear his passionate notes,
And virgins, as unknown he passed, have pined
And wasted for fond love of his wild eyes.
The fire of those soft orbs has ceased to burn,
And Silence, too enamoured of that voice,   65
Locks its mute music in her rugged cell.

  By solemn vision, and bright silver dream,
His infancy was nurtured. Every sight
And sound from the vast earth and ambient air,
Sent to his heart its choicest impulses.   70
The fountains of divine philosophy
Fled not his thirsting lips, and all of great,
Or good, or lovely, which the sacred past
In truth or fable consecrates, he felt
And knew. When early youth had passed, he left   75
His cold fireside and alienated home
To seek strange truths in undiscovered lands.
Many a wide waste and tangled wilderness
Has lured his fearless steps; and he has bought
With his sweet voice and eyes, from savage men,   80
His rest and food. Nature's most secret steps
He like her shadow has pursued, where'er
The red volcano overcanopies
Its fields of snow and pinnacles of ice
With burning smoke, or where bitumen lakes   85
On black bare pointed islets ever beat
With sluggish surge, or where the secret caves
Rugged and dark, winding among the springs

Of fire and poison, inaccessible
To avarice or pride, their starry domes   90
Of diamond and of gold expand above
Numberless and immeasurable halls,
Frequent with crystal column, and clear shrines
Of pearl, and thrones radiant with chrysolite.
Nor had that scene of ampler majesty   95
Than gems of gold, the varying roof of heaven
And the green earth lost in his heart its claims
To love and wonder; he would linger long
In lonesome vales, making the wild his home,
Until the doves and squirrels would partake   100
From his innocuous hand his bloodless food,
Lured by the gentle meaning of his looks,
And the wild antelope, that starts whene'er
The dry leaf rustles in the brake, suspend
Her timid steps to gaze upon a form   105
More graceful than her own.
                         His wandering step
Obedient to high thoughts, has visited
The awful ruins of the days of old:
Athens, and Tyre, and Balbec, and the waste
Where stood Jerusalem, the fallen towers   110
Of Babylon, the eternal pyramids,
Memphis and Thebes, and whatsoe'er of strange
Sculptured on alabaster obelisk,
Or jasper tomb, or mutilated sphynx,
Dark Aethiopia in her desert hills   115
Conceals. Among the ruined temples there,
Stupendous columns, and wild images
Of more than man, where marble daemons watch
The Zodiac's brazen mystery, and dead men
Hang their mute thoughts on the mute walls around, 120
He lingered, poring on memorials

Of the world's youth, through the long burning day
Gazed on those speechless shapes, nor, when the moon
Filled the mysterious halls with floating shades
Suspended he that task, but ever gazed   125
And gazed, till meaning on his vacant mind
Flashed like strong inspiration, and he saw
   The thrilling secrets of the birth of time.

   (ii) *Death's rare and regal prey* (ll. 602–720)
   The dim and hornèd moon hung low, and poured
A sea of lustre on the horizon's verge   130
That overflowed its mountains. Yellow mist
Filled the unbounded atmosphere, and drank
Wan moonlight even to fulness: not a star
Shone, not a sound was heard; the very winds,
Dangers' grim playmates, on that precipice   135
Slept, clasped in his embrace.—O, storm of death!
Whose sightless speed divides this sullen night:
And thou, colossal Skeleton, that, still
Guiding its irresistible career
In thy devastating omnipotence,   140
Art king of this frail world, from the red field
Of slaughter, from the reeking hospital,
The patriot's sacred couch, the snowy bed
Of innocence, the scaffold and the throne,
A mighty voice invokes thee. Ruin calls   145
His brother Death. A rare and regal prey
He hath prepared, prowling around the world;
Glutted with which thou mayst repose, and men
Go to their graves like flowers or creeping worms,
Nor ever more offer at thy dark shrine   150
The unheeded tribute of a broken heart.

   When on the threshold of the green recess
The wanderer's footsteps fell, he knew that death

Was on him. Yet a little, ere it fled,
Did he resign his high and holy soul   155
To images of the majestic past,
That paused within his passive being now,
Like winds that bear sweet music, when they breathe
Through some dim latticed chamber. He did place
His pale lean hand upon the rugged trunk   160
Of the old pine. Upon an ivied stone
Reclined his languid head, his limbs did rest,
Diffused and motionless, on the smooth brink
Of that obscurest chasm;—and thus he lay,
Surrendering to their final impulses   165
The hovering powers of life. Hope and despair,
The torturers, slept; no mortal pain or fear
Marred his repose, the influxes of sense,
And his own being unalloyed by pain,
Yet feebler and more feeble, calmly fed   170
The stream of thought, till he lay breathing there
At peace, and faintly smiling:—his last sight
Was the great moon, which o'er the western line
Of the wide world her mighty horn suspended,
With whose dun beams inwoven darkness seemed   175
To mingle. Now upon the jaggéd hills
It rests, and still as the divided frame
Of the vast meteor sunk, the Poet's blood,
That ever beat in mystic sympathy
With nature's ebb and flow, grew feebler still: 180
And when two lessening points of light alone
Gleamed through the darkness, the alternate gasp
Of his faint respiration scarce did stir
The stagnate night:—till the minutest ray
Was quenched, the pulse yet lingered in his heart.   185
It paused—it fluttered. But when heaven remained
Utterly black, the murky shades involved

An image, silent, cold, and motionless,
As their own voiceless earth and vacant air.
Even as a vapour fed with golden beams   190
That ministered on sunlight, ere the west
Eclipses it, was now that wondrous frame—
No sense, no motion, no divinity—
A fragile lute, on whose harmonious strings
The breath of heaven did wander—a bright stream   195
Once fed with many-voicéd waves—a dream
Of youth, which night and time have quenched for ever,
Still, dark, and dry, and unremembered now.
    O, for Medea's wondrous alchemy,
Which wheresoe'er it fell made the earth gleam   200
With bright flowers, and the wintry boughs exhale
From vernal blooms fresh fragrance! O, that God,
Profuse of poisons, would concede the chalice
Which but one living man has drained, who now,
Vessel of deathless wrath, a slave that feels   205
No proud exemption in the blighting curse
He bears, over the world wanders for ever,
Lone as incarnate death! O, that the dream
Of dark magician in his visioned cave,
Raking the cinders of a crucible   210
For life and power, even when his feeble hand
Shakes in its last decay, were the true law
Of this so lovely world! But thou art fled
Like some frail exhalation; which the dawn
Robes in its golden beams,—ah! thou hast fled!   215
The brave, the gentle, and the beautiful,
The child of grace and genius. Heartless things
Are done and said i' the world, and many worms
And beasts and men live on, and mighty Earth
From sea and mountain, city and wilderness,   220
In vesper low or joyous orison,

Lifts still its solemn voice:—but thou art fled—
Thou canst no longer know or love the shapes
Of this phantasmal scene, who have to thee
Been purest ministers, who are, alas!   225
Now thou art not. Upon those pallid lips
So sweet even in their silence, on those eyes
That image sleep in death, upon that form
Yet safe from the worm's outrage, let no tear
Be shed—not even in thought. Nor, when those hues 230
Are gone, and those divinest lineaments,
Worn by the senseless wind, shall live alone
In the frail pauses of this simple strain,
Let not high verse, mourning the memory
Of that which is no more, or painting's woe   235
Or sculpture, speak in feeble imagery
Their own cold powers. Art and eloquence,
And all the shows o' the world are frail and vain
To weep a loss that turns their lights to shade.
It is a woe too 'deep for tears', when all   240
Is reft at once, when some surpassing Spirit,
Whose light adorned the world around it, leaves
Those who remain behind, not sobs or groans,
The passionate tumult of a clinging hope;
But pale despair and cold tranquillity,   245
Nature's vast frame, the web of human things,
Birth and the grave, that are not as they were.

From *Julian and Maddalo*

(Composed at Este, autumn 1818; first published in the
Posthumous Poems, 1824)

I RODE one evening with Count Maddalo
Upon the bank of land which breaks the flow
Of Adria towards Venice: a bare strand
Of hillocks, heaped from ever-shifting sand,
Matted with thistles and amphibious weeds,   5
Such as from earth's embrace the salt ooze breeds,
Is this; an uninhabited sea-side,
Which the lone fisher, when his nets are dried,
Abandons; and no other object breaks
The waste, but one dwarf tree and some few stakes   10
Broken and unrepaired, and the tide makes
A narrow space of level sand thereon,
Where 'twas our wont to ride while day went down.
This ride was my delight. I love all waste
And solitary places; where we taste   15
The pleasure of believing what we see
Is boundless, as we wish our souls to be:
And such was this wide ocean, and this shore
More barren than its billows; and yet more
Than all, with a remembered friend I love   20
To ride as then I rode;—for the winds drove
The living spray along the sunny air
Into our faces; the blue heavens were bare,
Stripped to their depths by the awakening north;
And, from the waves, sound like delight broke forth   25
Harmonising with solitude, and sent
Into our hearts aëreal merriment.
So, as we rode, we talked; and the swift thought,
Winging itself with laughter, lingered not,

But flew from brain to brain,—such glee was ours,   30
Charged with light memories of remembered hours,
None slow enough for sadness: till we came
Homeward, which always makes the spirit tame.
This day had been cheerful but cold, and now
The sun was sinking, and the wind also.   35
Our talk grew somewhat serious, as may be
Talk interrupted with such raillery
As mocks itself, because it cannot scorn
The thoughts it would extinguish:—'twas forlorn,
Yet pleasing, such as once, so poets tell,   40
The devils held within the dales of Hell
Concerning God, freewill and destiny:
Of all that earth has been or yet may be,
All that vain men imagine or believe,
Or hope can paint or suffering may achieve,   45
We descanted, and I (for ever still
Is it not wise to make the best of ill?)
Argued against despondency, but pride
Made my companion take the darker side.
The sense that he was greater than his kind   50
Had struck, methinks, his eagle spirit blind
By gazing on its own exceeding light.
Meanwhile the sun paused ere it should alight,
Over the horizon of the mountains;—Oh,
How beautiful is sunset, when the glow   55
Of Heaven descends upon a land like thee,
Thou Paradise of exiles, Italy!
The mountains, seas, and vineyards, and the towers
Of cities they encircle!—it was ours
To stand on thee, beholding it: and then,   60
Just where we had dismounted, the Count's men
Were waiting for us with the gondola.—
As those who pause on some delightful way

Though bent on pleasant pilgrimage, we stood
Looking upon the evening, and the flood 65
Which lay between the city and the shore,
Paved with the image of the sky . . . the hoar
And aëry Alps towards the North appeared
Through mist, an heaven-sustaining bulwark reared
Between the East and West; and half the sky 70
Was roofed with clouds of rich emblazonry
Dark purple at the zenith, which still grew
Down the steep West into a wondrous hue
Brighter than burning gold, even to the rent
Where the swift sun yet paused in his descent 75
Among the many-folded hills: they were
Those famous Euganean hills, which bear,
As seen from Lido thro' the harbour piles,
The likeness of a clump of peakèd isles—
And then—as if the Earth and Sea had been 80
Dissolved into one lake of fire, were seen
Those mountains towering as from waves of flame
Around the vaporous sun, from which there came
The inmost purple spirit of light, and made
Their very peaks transparent. 'Ere it fade,' 85
Said my companion, 'I will show you soon
A better station'—so, o'er the lagune
We glided; and from that funereal bark
I leaned, and saw the city, and could mark
How from their many isles, in evening's gleam, 90
Its temples and its palaces did seem
Like fabrics of enchantment piled to Heaven.
I was about to speak, when—'We are even
Now at the point I meant,' said Maddalo,
And bade the gondolieri cease to row. 95
'Look, Julian, on the west, and listen well
If you hear not a deep and heavy bell.'

I looked, and saw between us and the sun
A building on an island; such a one
As age to age might add, for uses vile,   100
A windowless, deformed and dreary pile;
And on the top an open tower, where hung
A bell, which in the radiance swayed and swung;
We could just hear its hoarse and iron tongue:
The broad sun sunk behind it, and it tolled   105
In strong and black relief.—'What we behold
Shall be the madhouse and its belfry tower,'
Said Maddalo, 'and ever at this hour
Those who may cross the water, hear that bell
Which calls the maniacs, each one from his cell,   110
To vespers.'—'As much skill as need to pray
In thanks or hope for their dark lot have they
To their stern maker,' I replied. 'O ho!
You talk as in years past,' said Maddalo.
''Tis strange men change not. You were ever still   115
Among Christ's flock a perilous infidel,
A wolf for the meek lambs—if you can't swim
Beware of Providence.' I looked on him,
But the gay smile had faded in his eye.
'And such,'—he cried, 'is our mortality,   120
And this must be the emblem and the sign
Of what should be eternal and divine!—
And like that black and dreary bell, the soul,
Hung in a heaven-illumined tower, must toll
Our thoughts and our desires to meet below   125
Round the rent heart and pray—as madmen do
For what? they know not,—till the night of death
As sunset that strange vision, severeth
Our memory from itself, and us from all
We sought and yet were baffled.' I recall   130
The sense of what he said, although I mar

The force of his expressions. The broad star
Of day meanwhile had sunk behind the hill,
And the black bell became invisible,
And the red tower looked gray, and all between   135
The churches, ships and palaces were seen
Huddled in gloom;—into the purple sea
The orange hues of heaven sunk silently.
We hardly spoke, and soon the gondola
Conveyed me to my lodging by the way.   140
The following morn was rainy, cold and dim:
Ere Maddalo arose, I called on him,
And whilst I waited with his child I played;
A lovelier toy sweet Nature never made,
A serious, subtle, wild, yet gentle being,   145
Graceful without design and unforeseeing,
With eyes—Oh speak not of her eyes!—which seem
Twin mirrors of Italian Heaven, yet gleam
With such deep meaning, as we never see
But in the human countenance: with me   150
She was a special favourite: I had nursed
Her fine and feeble limbs when she came first
To this bleak world; and she yet seemed to know
On second sight her ancient playfellow,
Less changed than she was by six months or so;   155
For after her first shyness was worn out
We sate there, rolling billiard balls about,
When the Count entered. Salutations past—
'The word you spoke last night might well have cast
A darkness on my spirit—if man be   160
The passive thing you say, I should not see
Much harm in the religions and old saws
(Tho' I may never own such leaden laws)
Which break a teachless nature to the yoke:
Mine is another faith'—thus much I spoke   165

And noting he replied not, added: 'See
This lovely child, blithe, innocent and free;
She spends a happy time with little care,
While we to such sick thoughts subjected are
As came on you last night—it is our will   170
That thus enchains us to permitted ill—
We might be otherwise—we might be all
We dream of happy, high, majestical.
Where is the love, beauty, and truth we seek
But in our mind? and if we were not weak   175
Should we be less in deed than in desire?'
'Ay, if we were not weak—and we aspire
How vainly to be strong!' said Maddalo:
'You talk Utopia.' 'It remains to know,'
I then rejoined, 'and those who try may find   180
How strong the chains are which our spirit bind;
Brittle perchance as straw . . . We are assured
Much may be conquered, much may be endured,
Of what degrades and crushes us. We know
That we have power over ourselves to do   185
And suffer—what, we know not till we try;
But something nobler than to live and die—
So taught those kings of old philosophy
Who reigned, before Religion made men blind;
And those who suffer with their suffering kind   190
Yet feel their faith, religion.' 'My dear friend,'
Said Maddalo, 'my judgement will not bend
To your opinion, though I think you might
Make such a system refutation-tight
As far as words go. I knew one like you   195
Who to this city came some months ago,
With whom I argued in this sort, and he
Is now gone mad,—and so he answered me,—
Poor fellow! but if you would like to go

We'll visit him, and his wild talk will show   200
How vain are such aspiring theories.'
'I hope to prove the induction otherwise,
And that a want of that true theory, still,
Which seeks a "soul of goodness" in things ill
Or in himself or others, has thus bowed   205
His being—there are some by nature proud,
Who patient in all else demand but this—
To love and be beloved with gentleness;
And being scorned, what wonder if they die
Some living death? this is not destiny   210
But man's own wilful ill.'

Lines written among the Euganean Hills

(Composed at Este, October 1818; published with *Rosalind and Helen*, 1819)

MANY a green isle needs must be
In the deep wide sea of Misery,
Or the mariner, worn and wan,
Never thus could voyage on—
Day and night, and night and day,   5
Drifting on his dreary way,
With the solid darkness black
Closing round his vessel's track;
Whilst above the sunless sky,
Big with clouds, hangs heavily,   10
And behind the tempest fleet
Hurries on with lightning feet,
Riving sail, and cord, and plank,
Till the ship has almost drank
Death from the o'er-brimming deep;   15
And sinks down, down, like that sleep

When the dreamer seems to be
Weltering through eternity;
And the dim low line before
Of a dark and distant shore   20
Still recedes, as ever still
Longing with divided will,
But no power to seek or shun,
He is ever drifted on
O'er the unreposing wave   25
To the haven of the grave.
What, if there no friends will greet;
What, if there no heart will meet
His with love's impatient beat;
Wander wheresoe'er he may,   30
Can he dream before that day
To find refuge from distress
In friendship's smile, in love's caress?
Then 'twill wreak him little woe
Whether such there be or no: 35
Senseless is the breast, and cold,
Which relenting love would fold;
Bloodless are the veins and chill
Which the pulse of pain did fill;
Every little living nerve   40
That from bitter words did swerve
Round the tortured lips and brow,
Are like sapless leaflets now
Frozen upon December's bough.

On the beach of a northern sea   45
Which tempests shake eternally,
As once the wretch there lay to sleep,
Lies a solitary heap,
One white skull and seven dry bones,

On the margin of the stones, 50
Where a few gray rushes stand,
Boundaries of the sea and land:
Nor is heard one voice of wail
But the sea-mews, as they sail
O'er the billows of the gale; 55
Or the whirlwind up and down
Howling, like a slaughtered town,
When a king in glory rides
Through the pomp of fratricides:
Those unburied bones around 60
There is many a mournful sound;
There is no lament for him,
Like a sunless vapour, dim,
Who once clothed with life and thought
What now moves nor murmurs not. 65

Ay, many flowering islands lie
In the waters of wide Agony:
To such a one this morn was led,
My bark by soft winds piloted:
'Mid the mountains Euganean 70
I stood listening to the paean
With which the legioned rooks did hail
The sun's uprise majestical;
Gathering round with wings all hoar,
Through the dewy mist they soar 75
Like gray shades, till the eastern heaven
Bursts, and then, as clouds of even,
Flecked with fire and azure, lie
In the unfathomable sky,
So their plumes of purple grain, 80
Starred with drops of golden rain,
Gleam above the sunlight woods,

As in silent multitudes
On the morning's fitful gale
Through the broken mist they sail,   85
And the vapours cloven and gleaming
Follow, down the dark steep streaming,
Till all is bright, and clear, and still,
Round the solitary hill.

Beneath is spread like a green sea   90
The waveless plain of Lombardy,
Bounded by the vaporous air,
Islanded by cities fair;
Underneath Day's azure eyes
Ocean's nursling, Venice lies,   95
A peopled labyrinth of walls,
Amphitrite's destined halls,
Which her hoary sire now paves
With his blue and beaming waves.
Lo! the sun upsprings behind,   100
Broad, red, radiant, half-reclined
On the level quivering line
Of the waters crystalline;
And before that chasm of light,
As within a furnace bright,   105
Column, tower, and dome, and spire,
Shine like obelisks of fire,
Pointing with inconstant motion
From the altar of dark ocean
To the sapphire-tinted skies;   110
As the flames of sacrifice
From the marble shrines did rise,
As to pierce the dome of gold
Where Apollo spoke of old.

Sun-girt City, thou hast been 115
Ocean's child, and then his queen;
Now is come a darker day,
And thou soon must be his prey,
If the power that raised thee here
Hallow so thy watery bier. 120
A less drear ruin then than now,
With thy conquest-branded brow
Stooping to the slave of slaves
From thy throne, among the waves
Wilt thou be, when the sea-mew 125
Flies, as once before it flew,
O'er thine isles depopulate,
And all is in its ancient state,
Save where many a palace gate
With green sea-flowers overgrown 130
Like a rock of Ocean's own,
Topples o'er the abandoned sea
As the tides change sullenly.
The fisher on his watery way,
Wandering at the close of day, 135
Will spread his sail and seize his oar
Till he pass the gloomy shore,
Lest thy dead should, from their sleep
Bursting o'er the starlight deep,
Lead a rapid masque of death 140
O'er the waters of his path.

Those who alone thy towers behold
Quivering through aëreal gold,
As I now behold them here,
Would imagine not they were 145
Sepulchres, where human forms,
Like pollution-nourished worms,

To the corpse of greatness cling,
Murdered, and now mouldering:
But if Freedom should awake   150
In her omnipotence, and shake
From the Celtic Anarch's hold
All the keys of dungeons cold,
Where a hundred cities lie
Chained like thee, ingloriously,   155
Thou and all thy sister band
Might adorn this sunny land,
Twining memories of old time
With new virtues more sublime;
If not, perish thou and they!—   160
Clouds which stain truth's rising day
By her sun consumed away—
Earth can spare ye: while like flowers,
In the waste of years and hours,
From your dust new nations spring   165
With more kindly blossoming.

Perish—let there only be
Floating o'er thy hearthless sea
As the garment of thy sky
Clothes the world immortally,   170
One remembrance, more sublime
Than the tattered pall of time,
Which scarce hides thy visage wan;—
That a tempest-cleaving Swan
Of the songs of Albion,   175
Driven from his ancestral streams
By the might of evil dreams,
Found a nest in thee; and Ocean
Welcomed him with such emotion
That its joy grew his, and sprung   180

From his lips like music flung
O'er a mighty thunder-fit,
Chastening terror:—what though yet
Poesy's unfailing River,
Which through Albion winds forever   185
Lashing with melodious wave
Many a sacred Poet's grave,
Mourn its latest nursling fled?
What though thou with all thy dead
Scarce can for this fame repay   190
Aught thine own? oh, rather say
Though thy sins and slaveries foul
Overcloud a sunlike soul?
As the ghost of Homer clings
Round Scamander's wasting springs;   195
As divinest Shakespeare's might
Fills Avon and the world with light
Like omniscient power which he
Imaged 'mid mortality;
As the love from Petrarch's urn,   200
Yet amid yon hills doth burn,
A quenchless lamp by which the heart
Sees things unearthly;—so thou art,
Mighty spirit—so shall be
The City that did refuge thee.   205

Lo, the sun floats up the sky
Like thought-wingèd Liberty,
Till the universal light
Seems to level plain and height;
From the sea a mist has spread,   210
And the beams of morn lie dead
On the towers of Venice now,
Like its glory long ago.

By the skirts of that gray cloud
Many-domèd Padua proud   215
Stands, a peopled solitude,
'Mid the harvest-shining plain,
Where the peasant heaps his grain
In the garner of his foe,
And the milk-white oxen slow   220
With the purple vintage strain,
Heaped upon the creaking wain,
That the brutal Celt may swill
Drunken sleep with savage will;
And the sickle to the sword   225
Lies unchanged, though many a lord,
Like a weed whose shade is poison,
Overgrows this region's foison,
Sheaves of whom are ripe to come
To destruction's harvest-home: 230
Men must reap the things they sow,
Force from force must ever flow,
Or worse; but 'tis a bitter woe
That love or reason cannot change
The despot's rage, the slave's revenge.   235
Padua, thou within whose walls
Those mute guests at festivals,
Son and Mother, Death and Sin,
Played at dice for Ezzelin,
Till Death cried, 'I win, I win!'   240
And Sin cursed to lose the wager,
But Death promised, to assuage her,
That he would petition for
Her to be made Vice-Emperor,
When the destined years were o'er,   245
Over all between the Po
And the eastern Alpine snow,

Under the mighty Austrian.
Sin smiled so as Sin only can,
And since that time, ay, long before,   250
Both have ruled from shore to shore,—
That incestuous pair, who follow
Tyrants as the sun the swallow,
As Repentance follows Crime,
And as changes follow Time.   255

In thine halls the lamp of learning,
Padua, now no more is burning;
Like a meteor, whose wild way
Is lost over the grave of day,
It gleams betrayed and to betray: 260
Once remotest nations came
To adore that sacred flame,
When it lit not many a hearth
On this cold and gloomy earth:
Now new fires from antique light   265
Spring beneath the wide world's might;
But their spark lies dead in thee,
Trampled out by Tyranny.
As the Norway woodman quells,
In the depth of piny dells,   270
One light flame among the brakes,
While the boundless forest shakes,
And its mighty trunks are torn
By the fire thus lowly born:
The spark beneath his feet is dead,   275
He starts to see the flames it fed
Howling through the darkened sky
With a myriad tongues victoriously,
And sinks down in fear: so thou,
O Tyranny, beholdest now   280

Light around thee, and thou hearest
The loud flames ascend, and fearest:
Grovel on the earth; ay, hide
In the dust thy purple pride!

Noon descends around me now: 285
'Tis the noon of autumn's glow,
When a soft and purple mist
Like a vaporous amethyst,
Or an air-dissolvèd star
Mingling light and fragrance, far   290
From the curved horizon's bound
To the point of Heaven's profound,
Fills the overflowing sky;
And the plains that silent lie
Underneath, the leaves unsodden   295
Where the infant Frost has trodden
With his morning-wingèd feet,
Whose bright print is gleaming yet;
And the red and golden vines,
Piercing with their trellised lines   300
The rough, dark-skirted wilderness;
The dun and bladed grass no less,
Pointing from this hoary tower
In the windless air; the flower
Glimmering at my feet; the line   305
Of the olive-sandalled Apennine
In the south dimly islanded;
And the Alps, whose snows are spread
High between the clouds and sun;
And of living things each one;   310
And my spirit which so long
Darkened this swift stream of song,—
Interpenetrated lie

By the glory of the sky:
Be it love, light, harmony,   315
Odour, or the soul of all
Which from Heaven like dew doth fall,
Or the mind which feeds this verse
Peopling the lone universe.

Noon descends, and after noon   320
Autumn's evening meets me soon,
Leading the infantine moon,
And that one star, which to her
Almost seems to minister
Half the crimson light she brings   325
From the sunsets' radiant springs:
And the soft dreams of the morn
(Which like wingèd winds had borne
To that silent isle, which lies
Mid remembered agonies,   330
The frail bark of this lone being)
Pass, to other sufferers fleeing,
And its ancient pilot, Pain,
Sits beside the helm again.

Other flowering isles must be   335
In the sea of Life and Agony:
Other spirits float and flee
O'er that gulf: even now, perhaps,
On some rock the wild wave wraps,
With folded wings they waiting sit   340
For my bark, to pilot it
To some calm and blooming cove,
Where for me, and those I love,
May a windless bower be built,
Far from passion, pain, and guilt,   345

In a dell mid lawny hills,
Which the wild sea-murmur fills,
And soft sunshine, and the sound
Of old forests echoing round,
And the light and smell divine   350
Of all flowers that breathe and shine:
We may live so happy there,
That the Spirits of the Air,
Envying us, may even entice
To our healing Paradise   355
The polluting multitude;
But their rage would be subdued
By that clime divine and calm,
And the winds whose wings rain balm
On the uplifted soul, and leaves   360
Under which the bright sea heaves;
While each breathless interval
In their whisperings musical
The inspired soul supplies
With its own deep melodies,   365
And the love which heals all strife
Circling, like the breath of life,
All things in that sweet abode
With its own mild brotherhood:
They, not it, would change; and soon   370
Every sprite beneath the moon
Would repent its envy vain,
And the earth grow young again.

From *Prometheus Unbound*

(Composed at Este, September and October 1818 (Act I); at Rome March–April 6, 1819 (Acts II, III); at Florence close of 1819 (Act IV). Published 1820)

(i) *The chastened Titan*, Act I, ll. 1–73, 302–5

ACT I

Scene.—*A Ravine of Icy Rocks in the Indian Caucasus.* Prometheus *is discovered bound to the Precipice.* Panthea
and Ione *are seated at his feet. Time, night. During the
Scene, morning slowly breaks.*

Prometheus. Monarch of Gods and Dæmons, and all Spirits
But One, who throng those bright and rolling worlds
Which Thou and I alone of living things
Behold with sleepless eyes! regard this Earth
Made multitudinous with thy slaves, whom thou   5
Requitest for knee-worship, prayer, and praise,
And toil, and hecatombs of broken hearts,
With fear and self-contempt and barren hope.
Whilst me, who am thy foe, eyeless in hate,
Hast thou made reign and triumph, to thy scorn,   10
O'er mine own misery and thy vain revenge.
‛Three thousand years of sleep-unsheltered hours,
And moments aye divided by keen pangs
Till they seemed years, torture and solitude,
Scorn and despair,—these are mine empire:—   15
More glorious far than that which thou surveyest
From thine unenvied throne, O Mighty God!
Almighty, had I deigned to share the shame
Of thine ill tyranny, and hung not here
Nailed to this wall of eagle-baffling mountain,   20
Black, wintry, dead, unmeasured; without herb,

Insect, or beast, or shape or sound of life.
Ah me! alas, pain, pain ever, for ever!

No change, no pause, no hope! Yet I endure.
I ask the Earth, have not the mountains felt?   25
I ask yon Heaven, the all-beholding Sun,
Has it not seen? The Sea, in storm or calm,
Heaven's ever-changing Shadow, spread below,
Have its deaf waves not heard my agony?
Ah me! alas, pain, pain ever, for ever!   30

The crawling glaciers pierce me with the spears
Of their moon-freezing crystals, the bright chains
Eat with their burning cold into my bones.
Heaven's wingèd hound, polluting from thy lips
His beak in poison not his own, tears up   35
My heart; and shapeless sights come wandering by,
The ghastly people of the realm of dream,
Mocking me: and the Earthquake-fiends are charged
To wrench the rivets from my quivering wounds
When the rocks split and close again behind: 40
While from their loud abysses howling throng
The genii of the storm, urging the rage
Of whirlwind, and afflict me with keen hail.
And yet to me welcome is day and night,
Whether one breaks the hoar frost of the morn,   45
Or starry, dim, and slow, the other climbs
The leaden-coloured east; for then they lead
The wingless, crawling hours, one among whom
—As some dark Priest hales the reluctant victim—
Shall drag thee, cruel King, to kiss the blood   50
From these pale feet, which then might trample thee
If they disdained not such a prostrate slave.
Disdain! Ah no! I pity thee. What ruin

Will hunt thee undefended through wide Heaven!
How will thy soul, cloven to its depth with terror,   55
Gape like a hell within! I speak in grief,
Not exultation, for I hate no more,
As then ere misery made me wise. The curse
Once breathed on thee I would recall. Ye Mountains,
Whose many-voicèd Echoes, through the mist   60
Of cataracts, flung the thunder of that spell!
Ye icy Springs, stagnant with wrinkling frost,
Which vibrated to hear me, and then crept
Shuddering through India! Thou serenest Air,
Through which the Sun walks burning without beams!   65
And ye swift Whirlwinds, who on poisèd wings
Hung mute and moveless o'er yon hushed abyss,
As thunder, louder than your own, made rock
The orbèd world! If then my words had power,
Though I am changed so that aught evil wish   70
Is dead within; although no memory be
Of what is hate, let them not lose it now!
What was that curse? for ye all heard me speak.

[*The curse is repeated*]

Prometheus. Were these my words, O Parent?
The Earth.   They were thine.
Prometheus. It doth repent me: words are quick and vain;
Grief for awhile is blind, and so was mine.
I wish no living thing to suffer pain.   305

(ii) *The Poet*, Act I, ll. 737–51

On a poet's lips I slept
Dreaming like a love-adept
In the sound his breathing kept;
Nor seeks nor finds he mortal blisses,   740
But feeds on the aëreal kisses

Of shapes that haunt thought's wildernesses.
He will watch from dawn to gloom
The lake-reflected sun illume
The yellow bees in the ivy-bloom,   745
Nor heed nor see, what things they be;
But from these create he can
Forms more real than living man,
Nurslings of immortality!
One of these awakened me,   750
And I sped to succour thee.

(iii) *Song of Prometheus.* Act ii, scene v, ll. 48–71

Life of Life! thy lips enkindle
    With their love the breath between them;
And thy smiles before they dwindle
    Make the cold air fire; then screen them
In those looks, where whoso gazes
Faints, entangled in their mazes.

Child of Light! thy limbs are burning
    Through the vest which seems to hide them; 55
As the radiant lines of morning
    Through the clouds ere they divide them;
And this atmosphere divinest
Shrouds thee wheresoe'er thou shinest.

Fair are others; none beholds thee,   60
    But thy voice sounds low and tender
Like the fairest, for it folds thee
    From the sight, that liquid splendour,
And all feel, yet see thee never,
As I feel now, lost for ever!   65

Lamp of Earth! where'er thou movest
   Its dim shapes are clad with brightness,
And the souls of whom thou lovest
   Walk upon the winds with lightness,
Till they fail, as I am failing,   70
   Dizzy, lost, yet unbewailing!

(iv) *The Law of Life*, Act IV, ll. 554–78

This is the day, which down the void abysm
At the Earth-born's spell yawns for Heaven's despotism,
   And Conquest is dragged captive through the deep: 556
Love, from its awful throne of patient power
In the wise heart, from the last giddy hour
   Of dread endurance, from the slippery, steep,
And narrow verge of crag-like agony, springs   560
And folds over the world its healing wings.

Gentleness, Virtue, Wisdom, and Endurance,
These are the seals of that most firm assurance
   Which bars the pit over Destructions' strength;
And if, with infirm hand, Eternity,   565
Mother of many acts and hours, should free
   The serpent that would clasp her with his length;
These are the spells by which to reassume
An empire o'er the disentangled doom.

To suffer woes which Hope thinks infinite;   570
To forgive wrongs darker than death or night;
   To defy Power, which seems omnipotent;
To love, and bear; to hope till Hope creates
From its own wreck the thing it contemplates;
   Neither to change, nor falter, nor repent;   575
This, like thy glory, Titan, is to be
Good, great and joyous, beautiful and free;
This is alone Life, Joy, Empire, and Victory.

From the *Letter to Maria Gisborne*

(Composed at Leghorn, July 1820; published 1824)

You are now

In London, that great sea, whose ebb and flow
At once is deaf and loud, and on the shore
Vomits its wrecks, and still howls on for more.
Yet in its depth what treasures! You will see   5
That which was Godwin,—greater none than he
Though fallen—and fallen on evil times—to stand
Among the spirits of our age and land,
Before the dread tribunal of *to come*
The foremost,—while Rebuke cowers pale and dumb.   10
You will see Coleridge—he who sits obscure
In the exceeding lustre and the pure
Intense irradiation of a mind,
Which, with its own internal lightning blind,
Flags wearily through darkness and despair—   15
A cloud-encircled meteor of the air,
A hooded eagle among blinking owls.—
You will see Hunt—one of those happy souls
Which are the salt of the earth, and without whom
This world would smell like what it is—a tomb;   20
Who is, what others seem; his room no doubt
Is still adorned with many a cast from Shout,
With graceful flowers tastefully placed about;
And coronals of bay from ribbons hung,
And brighter wreaths in neat disorder flung;   25
The gifts of the most learned among some dozens
Of female friends, sisters-in-law, and cousins.
And there is he with his eternal puns,

Which beat the dullest brain for smiles, like duns
Thundering for money at a poet's door;   30
Alas! it is no use to say, 'I'm poor!'
Or oft in graver mood, when he will look
Things wiser than were ever read in book,
Except in Shakespeare's wisest tenderness.—
You will see Hogg,—and I cannot express   35
His virtues,—though I know that they are great,
Because he locks, then barricades the gate
Within which they inhabit;—of his wit
And wisdom, you'll cry out when you are bit.
He is a pearl within an oyster shell,   40
One of the richest of the deep;—and there
Is English Peacock, with his mountain Fair,
Turned into a Flamingo;—that shy bird
That gleams i' the Indian air—have you not heard
When a man marries, dies, or turns Hindoo,   45
His best friends hear no more of him?—but you
Will see him, and will like him too, I hope,
With the milk-white Snowdonian Antelope
Matched with this cameleopard—his fine wit
Makes such a wound, the knife is lost in it;   50
A strain too learnèd for a shallow age,
Too wise for selfish bigots; let his page,
Which charms the chosen spirits of the time,
Fold itself up for the serener clime
Of years to come, and find its recompense   55
In that just expectation.—Wit and sense,
Virtue and human knowledge; all that might
Make this dull world a business of delight,
Are all combined in Horace Smith.—And these,
With some exceptions, which I need not tease   60
Your patience by descanting on,—are all
You and I know in London.

I recall

My thoughts, and bid you look upon the night.
As water does a sponge, so the moonlight
Fills the void, hollow, universal air—   65
What see you?—unpavilioned Heaven is fair,
Whether the moon, into her chamber gone.
Leaves midnight to the golden stars, or wan
Climbs with diminished beams the azure steep;
Or whether clouds sail o'er the inverse deep,   70
Piloted by the many-wandering blast,
And the rare stars rush through them dim and fast:—
All this is beautiful in every land.—
But what see you beside?—a shabby stand
Of Hackney coaches—a brick house or wall   75
Fencing some lonely court, white with the scrawl
Of our unhappy politics;—or worse—
A wretched woman reeling by, whose curse
Mixed with the watchman's, partner of her trade,
You must accept in place of serenade—   80
Or yellow-haired Pollonia murmuring
To Henry, some unutterable thing.
I see a chaos of green leaves and fruit
Built round dark caverns, even to the root
Of the living stems that feed them—in whose bowers 85
There sleep in their dark dew the folded flowers;
Beyond, the surface of the unsickled corn
Trembles not in the slumbering air, and borne
In circles quaint, and ever-changing dance,
Like wingèd stars the fire-flies flash and glance,   90
Pale in the open moonshine, but each one
Under the dark trees seems a little sun,
A meteor tamed; a fixed star gone astray
From the silver regions of the milky way;—
Afar the Contadino's song is heard,   95

Rude, but made sweet by distance—and a bird
Which cannot be the Nightingale, and yet
I know none else that sings so sweet as it
At this late hour;—and then all is still—
Now—Italy or London, which you will!   100

From *Epipsychidion*

(Composed at Pisa, January, February 1821; published
summer 1822)

(i) *The Wonder of Love*

She met me, Stranger, upon life's rough way,
And lured me towards sweet Death; as Night by Day,
Winter by Spring, or Sorrow by swift Hope,
Led into light, life, peace. An antelope,
In the suspended impulse of its lightness,   5
Were less aethereally light: the brightness
Of her divinest presence trembles through
Her limbs, as underneath a cloud of dew
Embodied in the windless heaven of June
Amid the splendour-wingèd stars, the Moon   10
Burns, inextinguishably beautiful:
And from her lips, as from a hyacinth full
Of honey-dew, a liquid murmur drops,
Killing the sense with passion; sweet as stops
Of planetary music heard in trance.   15
In her mild lights the starry spirits dance,
The sunbeams of those wells which ever leap
Under the lightnings of the soul—too deep
For the brief fathom-line of thought or sense.
The glory of her being, issuing thence,   20
Stains the dead, blank, cold air with a warm shade

Of unentangled intermixture, made
By Love, of light and motion: one intense
Diffusion, one serene Omnipresence,
Whose flowing outlines mingle in their flowing,   25
Around her cheeks and utmost fingers glowing
With the unintermitted blood, which there
Quivers, (as in a fleece of snow-like air
The crimson pulse of living morning quiver,)
Continuously prolonged, and ending never,   30
Till they are lost, and in that Beauty furled
Which penetrates and clasps and fills the world;
Scarce visible from extreme loveliness.
Warm fragrance seems to fall from her light dress
And her loose hair; and where some heavy tress   35
The air of her own speed has disentwined,
The sweetness seems to satiate the faint wind;
And in the soul a wild odour is felt,
Beyond the sense, like fiery dews that melt
Into the bosom of a frozen bud.—   40
See where she stands! a mortal shape indued
With love and life and light and deity,
And motion which may change but cannot die;
An image of some bright Eternity;
A shadow of some golden dream; a Splendour   45
Leaving the third sphere pilotless; a tender
Reflection of the eternal Moon of Love
Under whose motions life's dull billows move;
A Metaphor of Spring and Youth and Morning;
A Vision like incarnate April, warning,   50
With smiles and tears, Frost the Anatomy
Into his summer grave.
                Ah, woe is me!
What have I dared? where am I lifted? how
Shall I descend, and perish not? I know

That Love makes all things equal: I have heard   55
By mine own heart this joyous truth averred:
The spirit of the worm beneath the sod
In love and worship blends itself with God.

(ii) *Aphrodite, Urania and Pandemos*

There was a Being whom my spirit oft
Met on its visioned wanderings, far aloft,
In the clear golden prime of my youth's dawn,
Upon the fairy isles of sunny lawn,
Amid the enchanted mountains, and the caves   5
Of divine sleep, and on the air-like waves
Of wonder-level dream, whose tremulous floor
Paved her light steps;—on an imagined shore,
Under the gray beak of some promontory
She met me, robed in such exceeding glory,   10
That I beheld her not. In solitudes
Her voice came to me through the whispering woods,
And from the fountains, and the odours deep
Of flowers, which, like lips murmuring in their sleep
Of the sweet kisses which had lulled them there,   15
Breathed but of *her* to the enamoured air;
And from the breezes whether low or loud,
And from the rain of every passing cloud,
And from the singing of the summer-birds,
And from all sounds, all silence. In the words   20
Of antique verse and high romance,—in form,
Sound, colour—in whatever checks that Storm
Which with the shattered present chokes the past;
And in that best philosophy, whose taste
Makes this cold common hell, our life, a doom   25
As glorious as a fiery martyrdom;
Her Spirit was the harmony of truth.—
Then, from the caverns of my dreamy youth

I sprang, as one sandalled with plumes of fire,
And towards the lodestar of my one desire,   30
I flitted, like a dizzy moth, whose flight
Is as a dead leaf's in the owlet light,
When it would seek in Hesper's setting sphere
A radiant death, a fiery sepulchre,
As if it were a lamp of earthly flame.—   35
But She, whom prayers or tears then could not tame,
Passed, like a God throned on a wingèd planet,
Whose burning plumes to tenfold swiftness fan it,
Into the dreary cone of our life's shade;
And as a man with mighty loss dismayed,   40
I would have followed, though the grave between
Yawned like a gulf whose spectres are unseen:
When a voice said:—' O thou of hearts the weakest,
The phantom is beside thee whom thou seekest.'
Then I—' Where?'—the world's echo answered 'where?'
And in that silence, and in my despair,   46
I questioned every tongueless wind that flew
Over my tower of mourning, if it knew
Whither 'twas fled, this soul out of my soul;
And murmured names and spells which have control   50
Over the sightless tyrants of our fate;
But neither prayer nor verse could dissipate
The night which closed on her; nor uncreate
That world within this Chaos, mine and me,
Of which she was the veiled Divinity,   55
The world I say of thoughts that worshipped her:
And therefore I went forth, with hope and fear
And every gentle passion sick to death,
Feeding my course with expectation's breath,
Into the wintry forest of our life;   60
And struggling through its error with vain strife,
And stumbling in my weakness and my haste,

And half bewildered by new forms, I passed,
Seeking among those untaught foresters
If I could find one form resembling hers,   65
In which she might have masked herself from me.
There,—One, whose voice was venomed melody
Sate by a well, under blue nightshade bowers;
The breath of her false mouth was like faint flowers,
Her touch was as electric poison,—flame   70
Out of her looks into my vitals came,
And from her living cheeks and bosom flew
A killing air, which pierced like honey-dew
Into the core of my green heart, and lay
Upon its leaves; until, as hair grown gray   75
O'er a young brow, they hid its unblown prime
With ruins of unseasonable time.

(iii) *The Island Paradise*

Emily,

A ship is floating in the harbour now,
A wind is hovering o'er the mountain's brow;
There is a path on the sea's azure floor,
No keel has ever ploughed that path before;   5
The halcyons brood around the foamless isles;
The treacherous Ocean has forsworn its wiles;
The merry mariners are bold and free:
Say, my heart's sister, wilt thou sail with me?
Our bark is as an albatross, whose nest   10
Is a far Eden of the purple East;
And we between her wings will sit, while Night,
And Day, and Storm, and Calm, pursue their flight,
Our ministers, along the boundless Sea,
Treading each other's heels, unheededly.   15
It is an isle under Ionian skies,
Beautiful as a wreck of Paradise,

And, for the harbours are not safe and good,
This land would have remained a solitude
But for some pastoral people native there,   20
Who from the Elysian, clear, and golden air
Draw the last spirit of the age of gold,
Simple and spirited; innocent and bold.
The blue Aegean girds this chosen home,
With ever-changing sound and light and foam,   25
Kissing the sifted sands, and caverns hoar;
And all the winds wandering along the shore
Undulate with the undulating tide:
There are thick woods where sylvan forms abide;
And many a fountain, rivulet, and pond,   30
As clear as elemental diamond,
Or serene morning air; and far beyond,
The mossy tracks made by the goats and deer
(Which the rough shepherd treads but once a year)
Pierce into glades, caverns, and bowers, and halls   35
Built round with ivy, which the waterfalls
Illumining, with sound that never fails
Accompany the noonday nightingales;
And all the place is peopled with sweet airs;
The light clear element which the isle wears   40
Is heavy with the scent of lemon-flowers,
Which floats like mist laden with unseen showers,
And falls upon the eyelids like faint sleep;
And from the moss violets and jonquils peep,
And dart their arrowy odour through the brain   45
Till you might faint with that delicious pain.
And every motion, odour, beam, and tone,
With that deep music is in unison:
Which is a soul within the soul—they seem
Like echoes of an antenatal dream.—   50
It is an isle 'twixt Heaven, Air, Earth, and Sea,

Cradled, and hung in clear tranquillity;
Bright as that wandering Eden Lucifer,
Washed by the soft blue Oceans of young air.
It is a favoured place. Famine or Blight, 55
Pestilence, War and Earthquake, never light
Upon its mountain-peaks; blind vultures, they
Sail onward far upon their fatal way:
The wingèd storms, chanting their thunder-psalm
To other lands, leave azure chasms of calm 60
Over this isle, or weep themselves in dew,
From which its fields and woods ever renew
Their green and golden immortality.
And from the sea there rise, and from the sky
There fall, clear exhalations, soft and bright, 65
Veil after veil, each hiding some delight,
Which Sun or Moon or zephyr draw aside,
Till the isle's beauty, like a naked bride
Glowing at once with love and loveliness,
Blushes and trembles at its own excess: 70
Yet, like a buried lamp, a Soul no less
Burns in the heart of this delicious isle,
An atom of th' Eternal, whose own smile
Unfolds itself, and may be felt, not seen
O'er the gray rocks, blue waves, and forests green, 75
Filling their bare and void interstices.—
But the chief marvel of the wilderness
Is a lone dwelling, built by whom or how
None of the rustic island-people know:
'Tis not a tower of strength, though with its height 80
It overtops the woods; but, for delight,
Some wise and tender Ocean-King, ere crime
Had been invented, in the world's young prime,
Reared it, a wonder of that simple time,
An envy of the isles, a pleasure-house 85

Made sacred to his sister and his spouse.
It scarce seems now a wreck of human art,
But, as it were Titanic; in the heart
Of Earth having assumed its form, then grown
Out of the mountains, from the living stone,   90
Lifting itself in caverns light and high:
For all the antique and learnèd imagery
Has been erased, and in the place of it
The ivy and the wild-vine interknit
The volumes of their many-twining stems;   95
Parasite flowers illume with dewy gems
The lampless halls, and when they fade, the sky
Peeps through their winter-woof of tracery
With moonlight patches, or star atoms keen,
Or fragments of the day's intense serene;—   100
Working mosaic on their Parian floors.
And, day and night, aloof, from the high towers
And terraces, the Earth and Ocean seem
To sleep in one another's arms, and dream
Of waves, flowers, clouds, woods, rocks, and all that we 105
Read in their smiles, and call reality.

This isle and house are mine, and I have vowed
Thee to be lady of the solitude.—
And I have fitted up some chambers there
Looking towards the golden Eastern air,   110
And level with the living winds, which flow
Like waves above the living waves below.—
I have sent books and music there, and all
Those instruments with which high Spirits call
The future from its cradle, and the past   115
Out of its grave, and make the present last
In thoughts and joys which sleep, but cannot die,
Folded within their own eternity.

Our simple life wants little, and true taste
Hires not the pale drudge Luxury, to waste   120
The scene it would adorn, and therefore still,
Nature with all her children haunts the hill.
The ring-dove, in the embowering ivy, yet
Keeps up her love-lament, and the owls flit
Round the evening tower, and the young stars glance 125
Between the quick bats in their twilight dance;
The spotted deer bask in the fresh moonlight
Before our gate, and the slow, silent night
Is measured by the pants of their calm sleep.
Be this our home in life, and when years heap   130
Their withered hours, like leaves, on our decay,
Let us become the overhanging day,
The living soul of this Elysian isle,
Conscious, inseparable, one.

Adonais

(Composed at Pisa, June 1821 ; printed at Pisa, July 1821 ; included
by Mrs. Shelley in the *Poetical Works* of 1839)

I

I WEEP for Adonais—he is dead!
O, weep for Adonais! though our tears
Thaw not the frost which binds so dear a head!
And thou, sad Hour, selected from all years
To mourn our loss, rouse thy obscure compeers,   5
And teach them thine own sorrow, say: 'With me
Died Adonais; till the Future dares
Forget the Past, his fate and fame shall be
An echo and a light unto eternity!'

II

Where wert thou, mighty Mother, when he lay, 10
When thy Son lay, pierced by the shaft which flies
In darkness? where was lorn Urania
When Adonais died? With veilèd eyes,
'Mid listening Echoes, in her Paradise
She sate, while one, with soft enamoured breath, 15
Rekindled all the fading melodies,
With which, like flowers that mock the corse beneath,
He had adorned and hid the coming bulk of Death.

III

Oh, weep for Adonais—he is dead!
Wake, melancholy Mother, wake and weep! 20
Yet wherefore? Quench within their burning bed
Thy fiery tears, and let thy loud heart keep
Like his, a mute and uncomplaining sleep;
For he is gone, where all things wise and fair
Descend;—oh, dream not that the amorous Deep 25
Will yet restore him to the vital air;
Death feeds on his mute voice, and laughs at our despair.

IV

Most musical of mourners, weep again!
Lament anew, Urania!—He died,
Who was the Sire of an immortal strain, 30
Blind, old, and lonely, when his country's pride
The priest, the slave, and the liberticide
Trampled and mocked with many a loathèd rite
Of lust and blood; he went, unterrified,
Into the gulf of death; but his clear Sprite 35
Yet reigns o'er earth; the third among the sons of light.

V

Most musical of mourners, weep anew!
Not all to that bright station dared to climb;
And happier they their happiness who knew,
Whose tapers yet burn through that night of time   40
In which suns perished; others more sublime,
Struck by the envious wrath of man or god,
Have sunk, extinct in their refulgent prime;
And some yet live, treading the thorny road,
Which leads, through toil and hate, to Fame's serene
    abode.   45

VI

But now, thy youngest, dearest one, has perished—
The nursling of thy widowhood, who grew,
Like a pale flower by some sad maiden cherished,
And fed with true-love tears, instead of dew;
Most musical of mourners, weep anew!   50
Thy extreme hope, the loveliest and the last.
The bloom, whose petals nipped before they blew
Died on the promise of the fruit, is waste;
The broken lily lies—the storm is overpast.

VII

To that high Capital, where kingly Death   55
Keeps his pale court in beauty and decay,
He came; and bought, with price of purest breath,
A grave among the eternal.—Come away!
Haste, while the vault of blue Italian day
Is yet his fitting charnel-roof! while still   60
He lies, as if in dewy sleep he lay;
Awake him not! surely he takes his fill
Of deep and liquid rest, forgetful of all ill.

VIII

He will awake no more, oh, never more!—
Within the twilight chamber spreads apace   65
The shadow of white Death, and at the door
Invisible Corruption waits to trace
His extreme way to her dim dwelling-place;
The eternal Hunger sits, but pity and awe
Soothe her pale rage, nor dares she to deface   70
So fair a prey, till darkness, and the law
Of change, shall o'er his sleep the mortal curtain draw.

IX

Oh, weep for Adonais!—The quick Dreams,
The passion-wingèd Ministers of thought,
Who were his flocks, whom near the living streams   75
Of his young spirit he fed, and whom he taught
The love which was its music, wander not,—
Wander no more, from kindling brain to brain,
But droop there, whence they sprung; and mourn their lot
Round the cold heart, where, after their sweet pain,   80
They ne'er will gather strength, or find a home again.

X

And one with trembling hands clasps his cold head,
And fans him with her moonlight wings, and cries:
'Our love, our hope, our sorrow, is not dead;
See, on the silken fringe of his faint eyes,   85
Like dew upon a sleeping flower, there lies
A tear some Dream has loosened from his brain.'
Lost Angel of a ruined Paradise!
She knew not 'twas her own; as with no stain
She faded, like a cloud which had outwept its rain.   90

XI

One from a lucid urn of starry dew
Washed his light limbs as if embalming them;
Another clipped her profuse locks, and threw
The wreath upon him, like an anadem,
Which frozen tears instead of pearls begem;   95
Another in her wilful grief would break
Her bow and wingèd reeds, as if to stem
A greater loss with one which was more weak;
And dull the barbèd fire against his frozen cheek.

XII

Another Splendour on his mouth alit,   100
That mouth, whence it was wont to draw the breath
Which gave it strength to pierce the guarded wit,
And pass into the panting heart beneath
With lightning and with music: the damp death
Quenched its caress upon his icy lips;   105
And, as a dying meteor stains a wreath
Of moonlight vapour, which the cold night clips,
It flushed through his pale limbs, and passed to its eclipse.

XIII

And others came . . . Desires and Adorations,
Wingèd Persuasions and veiled Destinies,   110
Splendours, and Glooms, and glimmering Incarnations
Of hopes and fears, and twilight Phantasies;
And Sorrow, with her family of Sighs,
And Pleasure, blind with tears, led by the gleam
Of her own dying smile instead of eyes,   115
Came in slow pomp;—the moving pomp might seem
Like pageantry of mist on an autumnal stream.

XIV

All he had loved, and moulded into thought,
From shape, and hue, and odour, and sweet sound,
Lamented Adonais. Morning sought   120
Her eastern watch-tower, and her hair unbound,
Wet with the tears which should adorn the ground,
Dimmed the aëreal eyes that kindle day;
Afar the melancholy thunder moaned,
Pale Ocean in unquiet slumber lay,   125
And the wild Winds flew round, sobbing in their dismay.

XV

Lost Echo sits amid the voiceless mountains,
And feeds her grief with his remembered lay,
And will no more reply to winds or fountains,
Or amorous birds perched on the young green spray, 130
Or herdsman's horn, or bell at closing day;
Since she can mimic not his lips, more dear
Than those for whose disdain she pined away
Into a shadow of all sounds:—a drear
Murmur, between their songs, is all the woodmen hear. 135

XVI

Grief made the young Spring wild, and she threw down
Her kindling buds, as if she Autumn were,
Or they dead leaves; since her delight is flown,
For whom should she have waked the sullen year?
To Phoebus was not Hyacinth so dear   140
Nor to himself Narcissus, as to both
Thou, Adonais: wan they stand and sere
Amid the faint companions of their youth,
With dew all turned to tears; odour, to sighing ruth.

XVII

Thy spirit's sister, the lorn nightingale   145
Mourns not her mate with such melodious pain;
Not so the eagle, who like thee could scale
Heaven, and could nourish in the sun's domain
Her mighty youth with morning, doth complain,
Soaring and screaming round her empty nest,   150
As Albion wails for thee: the curse of Cain
Light on his head who pierced thy innocent breast,
And scared the angel soul that was its earthly guest!

XVIII

Ah, woe is me! Winter is come and gone,
But grief returns with the revolving year;   155
The airs and streams renew their joyous tone;
The ants, the bees, the swallows reappear;
Fresh leaves and flowers deck the dead Seasons' bier;
The amorous birds now pair in every brake,
And build their mossy homes in field and brere;   160
And the green lizard, and the golden snake,
Like unimprisoned flames, out of their trance awake.

XIX

Through wood and stream and field and hill and Ocean
A quickening life from the Earth's heart has burst
As it has ever done, with change and motion,   165
From the great morning of the world when first
God dawned on Chaos; in its stream immersed,
The lamps of Heaven flash with a softer light;
All baser things pant with life's sacred thirst;
Diffuse themselves; and spend in love's delight,   170
The beauty and the joy of their renewèd might.

XX

The leprous corpse, touched by this spirit tender,
Exhales itself in flowers of gentle breath;
Like incarnations of the stars, when splendour
Is changed to fragrance, they illumine death   175
And mock the merry worm that wakes beneath;
Nought we know dies. Shall that alone which knows
Be as a sword consumed before the sheath
By sightless lightning?—the intense atom glows
A moment, then is quenched in a most cold repose.   180

XXI

Alas! that all we loved of him should be,
But for our grief, as if it had not been,
And grief itself be mortal! Woe is me!
Whence are we, and why are we? of what scene
The actors or spectators? Great and mean   185
Meet massed in death, who lends what life must borrow.
As long as skies are blue, and fields are green,
Evening must usher night, night urge the morrow,
Month follow month with woe, and year wake year to
    sorrow.

XXII

He will awake no more, oh, never more!   190
'Wake thou,' cried Misery, 'childless Mother, rise
Out of thy sleep, and slake, in thy heart's core,
A wound more fierce than his, with tears and sighs.'
And all the Dreams that watched Urania's eyes,
And all the Echoes whom their sister's song   195
Had held in holy silence, cried: 'Arise!'
Swift as a Thought by the snake Memory stung,
From her ambrosial rest the fading Splendour sprung.

XXIII

She rose like an autumnal Night, that springs
Out of the East, and follows wild and drear   200
The golden Day, which, on eternal wings,
Even as a ghost abandoning a bier,
Had left the Earth a corpse. Sorrow and fear
So struck, so roused, so rapt Urania;
So saddened round her like an atmosphere   205
Of stormy mist; so swept her on her way
Even to the mournful place where Adonais lay.

XXIV

Out of her secret Paradise she sped,
Through camps and cities rough with stone, and steel,
And human hearts, which to her aery tread   210
Yielding not, wounded the invisible
Palms of her tender feet where'er they fell:
And barbèd tongues, and thoughts more sharp than they,
Rent the soft Form they never could repel,
Whose sacred blood, like the young tears of May,   215
Paved with eternal flowers that undeserving way.

XXV

In the death-chamber for a moment Death,
Shamed by the presence of that living Might,
Blushed to annihilation, and the breath
Revisited those lips, and Life's pale light   220
Flashed through those limbs, so late her dear delight.
'Leave me not wild and drear and comfortless,
As silent lightning leaves the starless night!
Leave me not!' cried Urania: her distress
Roused Death: Death rose and smiled, and met her vain
   caress.   225

XXVI

'Stay yet awhile! speak to me once again;
Kiss me, so long but as a kiss may live;
And in my heartless breast and burning brain
That word, that kiss, shall all thoughts else survive,
With food of saddest memory kept alive,   230
Now thou art dead, as if it were a part
Of thee, my Adonais! I would give
All that I am to be as thou now art!
But I am chained to Time, and cannot thence depart!

XXVII

'O gentle child, beautiful as thou wert,   235
Why didst thou leave the trodden paths of men
Too soon, and with weak hands though mighty heart
Dare the unpastured dragon in his den?
Defenceless as thou wert, oh, where was then
Wisdom the mirrored shield, or scorn the spear?   240
Or hadst thou waited the full cycle, when
Thy spirit should have filled its crescent sphere,
The monsters of life's waste had fled from thee like deer.

XXVIII

'The herded wolves, bold only to pursue;
The obscene ravens, clamorous o'er the dead;   245
The vultures to the conqueror's banner true
Who feed where Desolation first has fed,
And whose wings rain contagion;—how they fled,
When, like Apollo, from his golden bow
The Pythian of the age one arrow sped   250
And smiled!—The spoilers tempt no second blow,
They fawn on the proud feet that spurn them lying low.

XXIX

'The sun comes forth, and many reptiles spawn;
He sets, and each ephemeral insect then
Is gathered into death without a dawn,   255
And the immortal stars awake again;
So is it in the world of living men:
A godlike mind soars forth, in its delight
Making earth bare and veiling heaven, and when
It sinks, the swarms that dimmed or shared its light   260
Leave to its kindred lamps the spirit's awful night.'

XXX

Thus ceased she: and the mountain shepherds came,
Their garlands sere, their magic mantles rent;
The Pilgrim of Eternity, whose fame
Over his living head like Heaven is bent,   265
An early but enduring monument,
Came, veiling all the lightnings of his song
In sorrow; from her wilds Ierne sent
The sweetest lyrist of her saddest wrong,
And Love taught Grief to fall like music from his tongue. 270

XXXI

Midst others of less note, came one frail Form,
A phantom among men; companionless
As the last cloud of an expiring storm
Whose thunder is its knell; he, as I guess,
Had gazed on Nature's naked loveliness,   275
Actaeon-like, and now he fled astray
With feeble steps o'er the world's wilderness,
And his own thoughts, along that rugged way,
Pursued, like raging hounds, their father and their prey.

XXXII

A pardlike Spirit beautiful and swift—   280
A Love in desolation masked;—a Power
Girt round with weakness;—it can scarce uplift
The weight of the superincumbent hour;
It is a dying lamp, a falling shower,
A breaking billow;—even whilst we speak   285
Is it not broken? On the withering flower
The killing sun smiles brightly: on a cheek
The life can burn in blood, even while the heart may break.

XXXIII

His head was bound with pansies overblown,
And faded violets, white, and pied, and blue;   290
And a light spear topped with a cypress cone,
Round whose rude shaft dark ivy-tresses grew
Yet dripping with the forest's noonday dew,
Vibrated, as the ever-beating heart
Shook the weak hand that grasped it; of that crew 295
He came the last, neglected and apart;
A herd-abandoned deer struck by the hunter's dart.

XXXIV

All stood aloof, and at his partial moan
Smiled through their tears; well knew that gentle band
Who in another's fate now wept his own,   300
As in the accents of an unknown land
He sung new sorrow; sad Urania scanned
The Stranger's mien, and murmured: 'Who art thou?'
He answered not, but with a sudden hand
Made bare his branded and ensanguined brow,   305
Which was like Cain's or Christ's—oh! that it should be so!

XXXV

What softer voice is hushed over the dead?
Athwart what brow is that dark mantle thrown?
What form leans sadly o'er the white death-bed,
In mockery of monumental stone,   310
The heavy heart heaving without a moan?
If it be He, who, gentlest of the wise,
Taught, soothed, loved, honoured the departed one,
Let me not vex, with inharmonious sighs,
The silence of that heart's accepted sacrifice.   315

XXXVI

Our Adonais has drunk poison—oh!
What deaf and viperous murderer could crown
Life's early cup with such a draught of woe?
The nameless worm would now itself disown:
It felt, yet could escape, the magic tone   320
Whose prelude held all envy, hate, and wrong,
But what was howling in one breast alone,
Silent with expectation of the song,
Whose master's hand is cold, whose silver lyre unstrung.

XXXVII

Live thou, whose infamy is not thy fame!   325
Live! fear no heavier chastisement from me,
Thou noteless blot on a remembered name!
But be thyself, and know thyself to be!
And ever at thy season be thou free
To spill the venom when thy fangs o'erflow: 330
Remorse and Self-contempt shall cling to thee;
Hot Shame shall burn upon thy secret brow,
And like a beaten hound tremble thou shalt—as now.

XXXVIII

Nor let us weep that our delight is fled
Far from these carrion kites that scream below;   335
He wakes or sleeps with the enduring dead;
Thou canst not soar where he is sitting now.—
Dust to the dust! but the pure spirit shall flow
Back to the burning fountain whence it came,
A portion of the Eternal, which must glow   340
Through time and change, unquenchably the same,
Whilst thy cold embers choke the sordid hearth of shame.

XXXIX

Peace, peace! he is not dead, he doth not sleep—
He hath awakened from the dream of life—
'Tis we, who lost in stormy visions, keep   345
With phantoms an unprofitable strife,
And in mad trance, strike with our spirit's knife
Invulnerable nothings.—*We* decay
Like corpses in a charnel; fear and grief
Convulse us and consume us day by day,   350
And cold hopes swarm like worms within our living clay.

XL

He has outsoared the shadow of our night;
Envy and calumny and hate and pain,
And that unrest which men miscall delight,
Can touch him not and torture not again;   355
From the contagion of the world's slow stain
He is secure, and now can never mourn
A heart grown cold, a head grown gray in vain;
Nor, when the spirit's self has ceased to burn,
With sparkless ashes load an unlamented urn.   360

XLI

He lives, he wakes—'tis Death is dead, not he;
Mourn not for Adonais.—Thou young Dawn,
Turn all thy dew to splendour, for from thee
The spirit thou lamentest is not gone;
Ye caverns and ye forests, cease to moan!   365
Cease, ye faint flowers and fountains, and thou Air,
Which like a mourning veil thy scarf hadst thrown
O'er the abandoned Earth, now leave it bare
Even to the joyous stars which smile on its despair!

XLII

He is made one with Nature: there is heard   370
His voice in all her music, from the moan
Of thunder, to the song of night's sweet bird;
He is a presence to be felt and known
In darkness and in light, from herb and stone,
Spreading itself where'er that Power may move   375
Which has withdrawn his being to its own;
Which wields the world with never-wearied love,
Sustains it from beneath, and kindles it above.

XLIII

He is a portion of the loveliness
Which once he made more lovely: he doth bear   380
His part, while the one Spirit's plastic stress
Sweeps through the dull dense world, compelling there
All new successions to the forms they wear;
Torturing th' unwilling dross that checks its flight
To its own likeness, as each mass may bear;   385
And bursting in its beauty and its might
From trees and beasts and men into the Heaven's light.

XLIV

The splendours of the firmament of time
May be eclipsed, but are extinguished not;
Like stars to their appointed height they climb,   390
And death is a low mist which cannot blot
The brightness it may veil. When lofty thought
Lifts a young heart above its mortal lair,
And love and life contend in it, for what
Shall be its earthly doom, the dead live there   395
And move like winds of light on dark and stormy air.

XLV

The inheritors of unfulfilled renown
Rose from their thrones, built beyond mortal thought,
Far in the Unapparent. Chatterton
Rose pale,—his solemn agony had not   400
Yet faded from him; Sidney, as he fought
And as he fell and as he lived and loved
Sublimely mild, a Spirit without spot,
Arose; and Lucan, by his death approved:
Oblivion as they rose shrank like a thing reproved.   405

XLVI

And many more, whose names on Earth are dark,
But whose transmitted effluence cannot die
So long as fire outlives the parent spark,
Rose, robed in dazzling immortality.
'Thou art become as one of us,' they cry,   410
'It was for thee yon kingless sphere has long
Swung blind in unascended majesty,
Silent alone amid an Heaven of Song.
Assume thy wingèd throne, thou Vesper of our throng!'

XLVII

Who mourns for Adonais? Oh, come forth,   415
Fond wretch! and know thyself and him aright.
Clasp with thy panting soul the pendulous Earth;
As from a centre, dart thy spirit's light
Beyond all worlds, until its spacious might
Satiate the void circumference: then shrink   420
Even to a point within our day and night;
And keep thy heart light lest it make thee sink
When hope has kindled hope, and lured thee to the brink.

XLVIII

Or go to Rome, which is the sepulchre,
Oh, not of him, but of our joy: 'tis nought   425
That ages, empires, and religions there
Lie buried in the ravage they have wrought;
For such as he can lend,—they borrow not
Glory from those who made the world their prey;
And he is gathered to the kings of thought   430
Who waged contention with their time's decay,
And of the past are all that cannot pass away.

XLIX

Go thou to Rome,—at once the Paradise,
The grave, the city, and the wilderness;
And where its wrecks like shattered mountains rise, 435
And flowering weeds, and fragrant copses dress
The bones of Desolation's nakedness
Pass, till the spirit of the spot shall lead
Thy footsteps to a slope of green access
Where, like an infant's smile, over the dead   440
A light of laughing flowers along the grass is spread;

L

And gray walls moulder round, on which dull Time
Feeds, like slow fire upon a hoary brand;
And one keen pyramid with wedge sublime,
Pavilioning the dust of him who planned   445
This refuge for his memory, doth stand
Like flame transformed to marble; and beneath,
A field is spread, on which a newer band
Have pitched in Heaven's smile their camp of death,
Welcoming him we lose with scarce extinguished breath. 450

LI

Here pause: these graves are all too young as yet
To have outgrown the sorrow which consigned
Its charge to each; and if the seal is set,
Here, on one fountain of a mourning mind,
Break it not thou! too surely shalt thou find   455
Thine own well full, if thou returnest home,
Of tears and gall. From the world's bitter wind
Seek shelter in the shadow of the tomb.
What Adonais is, why fear we to become?

LII

The One remains, the many change and pass;   460
Heaven's light forever shines, Earth's shadows fly;
Life, like a dome of many-coloured glass,
Stains the white radiance of Eternity,
Until Death tramples it to fragments.—Die,
If thou wouldst be with that which thou dost seek!   465
Follow where all is fled!—Rome's azure sky,
Flowers, ruins, statues, music, words, are weak
The glory they transfuse with fitting truth to speak.

LIII

Why linger, why turn back, why shrink, my Heart?
Thy hopes are gone before: from all things here   470
They have departed; thou shouldst now depart!
A light is passed from the revolving year,
And man, and woman; and what still is dear
Attracts to crush, repels to make thee wither.
The soft sky smiles,—the low wind whispers near: 475
'Tis Adonais calls! oh, hasten thither,
No more let Life divide what Death can join together.

LIV

That Light whose smile kindles the Universe,
That Beauty in which all things work and move,
That Benediction which the eclipsing Curse   480
Of birth can quench not, that sustaining Love
Which through the web of being blindly wove
By man and beast and earth and air and sea,
Burns bright or dim, as each are mirrors of
The fire for which all thirst; now beams on me, 485
Consuming the last clouds of cold mortality.

LV

The breath whose might I have invoked in song
Descends on me; my spirit's bark is driven
Far from the shore, far from the trembling throng
Whose sails were never to the tempest given; 490
The massy earth and spherèd skies are riven!
I am borne darkly, fearfully, afar;
Whilst, burning through the inmost veil of Heaven,
The soul of Adonais, like a star,
Beacons from the abode where the Eternal are. 495

Choral Odes from *Hellas*

(Composed autumn 1821; first published 1822)

I

WORLDS on worlds are rolling ever
  From creation to decay,
 Like the bubbles on a river
  Sparkling, bursting, borne away.
  But they are still immortal   5
  Who, through birth's orient portal
And death's dark chasm hurrying to and fro,
  Clothe their unceasing flight
  In the brief dust and light
Gathered around their chariots as they go;   10
  New shapes they still may weave,
  New gods, new laws receive,
Bright or dim are they as the robes they last
  On Death's bare ribs had cast.

 A power from the unknown God,   15
  A Promethean conqueror, came;
Like a triumphal path he trod
  The thorns of death and shame.
  A mortal shape to him
  Was like the vapour dim   20
Which the orient planet animates with light;
  Hell, Sin, and Slavery came,
  Like bloodhounds mild and tame,
Nor preyed, until their Lord had taken flight;
  The moon of Mahomet   25
  Arose, and it shall set:
While blazoned as on Heaven's immortal noon
  The cross leads generations on.

Swift as the radiant shapes of sleep
  From one whose dreams are Paradise   30
Fly, when the fond wretch wakes to weep,
  And Day peers forth with her blank eyes ;
  So fleet, so faint, so fair,
  The Powers of earth and air
Fled from the folding-star of Bethlehem :   35
  Apollo, Pan, and Love,
  And even Olympian Jove
Grew weak, for killing Truth had glared on them ;
  Our hills and seas and streams,
  Dispeopled of their dreams,   40
Their waters turned to blood, their dew to tears,
  Wailed for the golden years.

II

THE world's great age begins anew,
  The golden years return,
The earth doth like a snake renew
  Her winter weeds outworn:
Heaven smiles, and faiths and empires gleam,   5
Like wrecks of a dissolving dream.

A brighter Hellas rears its mountains
  From waves serener far ;
A new Peneus rolls his fountains
  Against the morning star ;   10
Where fairer Tempes bloom, there sleep
Young Cyclads on a sunnier deep.

A loftier Argo cleaves the main,
  Fraught with a later prize ;
Another Orpheus sings again,   15
  And loves, and weeps, and dies ;

A new Ulysses leaves once more
Calypso for his native shore.

Oh, write no more the tale of Troy,
   If earth Death's scroll must be!   20
Nor mix with Laian rage the joy
   Which dawns upon the free:
Although a subtler Sphinx renew
Riddles of death Thebes never knew.

Another Athens shall arise,   25
   And to remoter time
Bequeath, like sunset to the skies,
   The splendour of its prime;
And leave, if nought so bright may live,
All earth can take or Heaven can give.   30

Saturn and Love their long repose
   Shall burst, more bright and good
Than all who fell, than One who rose,
   Than many unsubdued:
Not gold, not blood, their altar dowers,   35
But votive tears and symbol flowers.

Oh, cease! must hate and death return?
   Cease! must men kill and die?
Cease! drain not to its dregs the urn
   Of bitter prophecy.   40
The world is weary of the past,
Oh, might it die or rest at last!

Ozymandias

(Published in Hunt's *Examiner*, January 1818;
reprinted with *Rosalind and Helen*, 1819)

I MET a traveller from an antique land
Who said: Two vast and trunkless legs of stone
Stand in the desert . . . Near them, on the sand,
Half sunk, a shattered visage lies, whose frown,
And wrinkled lip, and sneer of cold command,   5
Tell that its sculptor well those passions read
Which yet survive, stamped on these lifeless things,
The hand that mocked them, and the heart that fed:
And on the pedestal these words appear:
'My name is Ozymandias, king of kings: 10
Look on my works, ye Mighty, and despair!'
Nothing beside remains. Round the decay
Of that colossal wreck, boundless and bare
The lone and level sands stretch far away.

To the Nile

(Composed 4 February 1818; first published in the
St. James's Magazine, March 1876)

MONTH after month the gathered rains descend
Drenching yon secret Aethiopian dells,
And from the desert's ice-girt pinnacles
Where Frost and Heat in strange embraces blend
On Atlas, fields of moist snow half depend.   5
Girt there with blasts and meteors Tempest dwells
By Nile's aëreal urn, with rapid spells
Urging those waters to their mighty end.

O'er Egypt's land of Memory floods are level
And they are thine, O Nile—and well thou knowest 10
That soul-sustaining airs and blasts of evil
And fruits and poisons spring where'er thou flowest.
Beware, O Man—for knowledge must to thee,
Like the great flood to Egypt, ever be.

Ode to the West Wind [1]

(Written 1819; published 1820)

I

O WILD West Wind, thou breath of Autumn's being,
Thou, from whose unseen presence the leaves dead
Are driven, like ghosts from an enchanter fleeing,

Yellow, and black, and pale, and hectic red,
Pestilence-stricken multitudes: O thou,   5
Who chariotest to their dark wintry bed

The wingèd seeds, where they lie cold and low,
Each like a corpse within its grave, until
Thine azure sister of the Spring shall blow

---

[1] This poem was conceived and chiefly written in a wood that skirts the Arno, near Florence, and on a day when that tempestuous wind, whose temperature is at once mild and animating, was collecting the vapours which pour down the autumnal rains. They began, as I foresaw, at sunset with a violent tempest of hail and rain, attended by that magnificent thunder and lightning peculiar to the Cisalpine regions.

The phenomenon alluded to at the conclusion of the third stanza is well known to naturalists. The vegetation at the bottom of the sea, of rivers, and of lakes, sympathizes with that of the land in the change of seasons, and is consequently influenced by the winds which announce it.—[SHELLEY'S NOTE.]

Her clarion o'er the dreaming earth, and fill   10
(Driving sweet buds like flocks to feed in air)
With living hues and odours plain and hill:

Wild Spirit, which art moving everywhere;
Destroyer and preserver; hear, oh, hear!

II

Thou on whose stream, mid the steep sky's commotion, 15
Loose clouds like earth's decaying leaves are shed,
Shook from the tangled boughs of Heaven and Ocean,

Angels of rain and lightning: there are spread
On the blue surface of thine aëry surge,
Like the bright hair uplifted from the head   20

Of some fierce Maenad, even from the dim verge
Of the horizon to the zenith's height,
The locks of the approaching storm. Thou dirge

Of the dying year, to which this closing night
Will be the dome of a vast sepulchre,   25
Vaulted with all thy congregated might

Of vapours, from whose solid atmosphere
Black rain, and fire, and hail will burst: oh, hear!

III

Thou who didst waken from his summer dreams
The blue Mediterranean, where he lay,   30
Lulled by the coil of his crystàlline streams,

Beside a pumice isle in Baiae's bay,
And saw in sleep old palaces and towers
Quivering within the wave's intenser day,

All overgrown with azure moss and flowers   35
So sweet, the sense faints picturing them! Thou
For whose path the Atlantic's level powers

Cleave themselves into chasms, while far below
The sea-blooms and the oozy woods which wear
The sapless foliage of the ocean, know   40

Thy voice, and suddenly grow gray with fear,
And tremble and despoil themselves: oh, hear!

IV

If I were a dead leaf thou mightest bear;
If I were a swift cloud to fly with thee;
A wave to pant beneath thy power, and share   45

The impulse of thy strength, only less free
Than thou, O uncontrollable! If even
I were as in my boyhood, and could be

The comrade of thy wanderings over Heaven,
As then, when to outstrip thy skiey speed   50
Scarce seemed a vision; I would ne'er have striven

As thus with thee in prayer in my sore need.
Oh, lift me as a wave, a leaf, a cloud!
I fall upon the thorns of life! I bleed!

A heavy weight of hours has chained and bowed   55
One too like thee: tameless, and swift, and proud.

V

Make me thy lyre, even as the forest is:
What if my leaves are falling like its own!
The tumult of thy mighty harmonies

Will take from both a deep, autumnal tone,   60
Sweet though in sadness. Be thou, Spirit fierce,
My spirit! Be thou me, impetuous one!

Drive my dead thoughts over the universe
Like withered leaves to quicken a new birth!
And, by the incantation of this verse,   65

Scatter, as from an unextinguished hearth
Ashes and sparks, my words among mankind!
Be through my lips to unawakened earth

The trumpet of a prophecy! O, Wind,
If Winter comes, can Spring be far behind?   70

To a Skylark

(Composed at Leghorn, 1820; printed with
Prometheus Unbound in the same year)

HAIL to thee, blithe Spirit!
    Bird thou never wert,
That from Heaven, or near it,
    Pourest thy full heart
In profuse strains of unpremeditated art.   5

    Higher still and higher
    From the earth thou springest
Like a cloud of fire;
    The blue deep thou wingest,
And singing still dost soar, and soaring ever singest.   10

    In the golden lightning
    Of the sunken sun,
O'er which clouds are bright'ning,
    Thou dost float and run;
Like an unbodied joy whose race is just begun.   15

    The pale purple even
    Melts around thy flight;
Like a star of Heaven,
    In the broad daylight
Thou art unseen, but yet I hear thy shrill delight,   20

Keen as are the arrows
   Of that silver sphere,
Whose intense lamp narrows
   In the white dawn clear
Until we hardly see—we feel that it is there.   25

All the earth and air
   With thy voice is loud,
As, when night is bare,
   From one lonely cloud
The moon rains out her beams, and Heaven is overflowed. 30

What thou art we know not;
   What is most like thee?
From rainbow clouds there flow not
   Drops so bright to see
As from thy presence showers a rain of melody.   35

Like a Poet hidden
   In the light of thought,
Singing hymns unbidden,
   Till the world is wrought
To sympathy with hopes and fears it heeded not: 40

Like a high-born maiden
   In a palace-tower,
Soothing her love-laden
   Soul in secret hour
With music sweet as love, which overflows her bower: 45

Like a glow-worm golden
   In a dell of dew,
Scattering unbeholden
   Its aëreal hue   49
Among the flowers and grass, which screen it from the view!

Like a rose embowered
    In its own green leaves,
By warm winds deflowered,
    Till the scent it gives
Makes faint with too much sweet those heavy-wingèd thieves:

Sound of vernal showers   56
    On the twinkling grass,
Rain-awakened flowers,
    All that ever was
Joyous, and clear, and fresh, thy music doth surpass: 60

Teach us, Sprite or Bird,
    What sweet thoughts are thine:
I have never heard
    Praise of love or wine
That panted forth a flood of rapture so divine.   65

Chorus Hymeneal,
    Or triumphant chant,
Matched with thine would be all
    But an empty vaunt,
A thing wherein we feel there is some hidden want.   70

What objects are the fountains
    Of thy happy strain?
What fields, or waves, or mountains?
    What shapes of sky or plain?
What love of thine own kind? what ignorance of pain?   75

With thy clear keen joyance
    Languor cannot be:
Shadow of annoyance
    Never came near thee:
Thou lovest—but ne'er knew love's sad satiety.   80

Waking or asleep,
   Thou of death must deem
Things more true and deep
   Than we mortals dream,
Or how could thy notes flow in such a crystal stream?   85

We look before and after,
   And pine for what is not:
Our sincerest laughter
   With some pain is fraught;
Our sweetest songs are those that tell of saddest thought. 90

Yet if we could scorn
   Hate, and pride, and fear;
If we were things born
   Not to shed a tear,
I know not how thy joy we ever should come near.   95

Better than all measures
   Of delightful sound,
Better than all treasures
   That in books are found,
Thy skill to poet were, thou scorner of the ground!   100

Teach me half the gladness
   That thy brain must know,
Such harmonious madness
   From my lips would flow
The world should listen then—as I am listening now.   105

The Cloud

(Published with *Prometheus Unbound*, 1820)

I BRING fresh showers for the thirsting flowers,
   From the seas and the streams;
I bear light shade for the leaves when laid
   In their noonday dreams.

From my wings are shaken the dews that waken   5
    The sweet buds every one,
When rocked to rest on their mother's breast,
    As she dances about the sun.
I wield the flail of the lashing hail,
    And whiten the green plains under,   10
And then again I dissolve it in rain,
    And laugh as I pass in thunder.

I sift the snow on the mountains below,
    And their great pines groan aghast;
And all the night 'tis my pillow white,   15
    While I sleep in the arms of the blast.
Sublime on the towers of my skiey bowers,
    Lightning my pilot sits;
In a cavern under is fettered the thunder,
    It struggles and howls at fits;   20
Over earth and ocean, with gentle motion,
    This pilot is guiding me,
Lured by the love of the genii that move
    In the depths of the purple sea;
Over the rills, and the crags, and the hills,   25
    Over the lakes and the plains,
Wherever he dream, under mountain or stream,
    The Spirit he loves remains;
And I all the while bask in Heaven's blue smile,
    Whilst he is dissolving in rains.   30

The sanguine Sunrise, with his meteor eyes,
    And his burning plumes outspread,
Leaps on the back of my sailing rack,
    When the morning star shines dead;
As on the jag of a mountain crag,   35
    Which an earthquake rocks and swings,

An eagle alit one moment may sit
    In the light of its golden wings.
And when Sunset may breathe, from the lit sea beneath,
    Its ardours of rest and of love,   40
And the crimson pall of eve may fall
    From the depth of Heaven above,
With wings folded I rest, on mine aëry nest,
    As still as a brooding dove.

That orbèd maiden with white fire laden,   45
    Whom mortals call the Moon,
Glides glimmering o'er my fleece-like floor,
    By the midnight breezes strewn;
And wherever the beat of her unseen feet,
    Which only the angels hear,   50
May have broken the woof of my tent's thin roof
    The stars peep behind her and peer;
And I laugh to see them whirl and flee,
    Like a swarm of golden bees,
When I widen the rent in my wind-built tent,   55
    Till the calm rivers, lakes, and seas,
Like strips of the sky fallen through me on high,
    Are each paved with the moon and these.

I bind the Sun's throne with a burning zone,
    And the Moon's with a girdle of pearl;   60
The volcanoes are dim, and the stars reel and swim,
    When the whirlwinds my banner unfurl.
From cape to cape, with a bridge-like shape,
    Over a torrent sea,
Sunbeam-proof, I hang like a roof,—   65
    The mountains its columns be,
The triumphal arch through which I march
    With hurricane, fire, and snow,

When the Powers of the air are chained to my chair,
    Is the million-coloured bow;   70
The sphere-fire above its soft colours wove,
    While the moist Earth was laughing below.

I am the daughter of Earth and Water,
    And the nursling of the Sky;
I pass through the pores of the ocean and shores;   75
    I change, but I cannot die.
For after the rain when with never a stain
    The pavilion of Heaven is bare,
And the winds and sunbeams with their convex gleams
    Build up the blue dome of air,   80
I silently laugh at my own cenotaph,
    And out of the caverns of rain,
Like a child from the womb, like a ghost from the tomb,
    I arise and unbuild it again.

Hymn of Apollo

(Written in 1820; published 1824)

I

THE sleepless Hours who watch me as I lie,
    Curtained with star-inwoven tapestries
From the broad moonlight of the sky,
    Fanning the busy dreams from my dim eyes,—
Waken me when their Mother, the gray Dawn   5
Tells them that dreams and that the moon is gone.

II

Then I arise, and climbing Heaven's blue dome,
    I walk over the mountains and the waves,
Leaving my robe upon the ocean foam;
    My footsteps pave the clouds with fire; the caves   10

Are filled with my bright presence, and the air
Leaves the green Earth to my embraces bare.

III

The sunbeams are my shafts, with which I kill
  Deceit, that loves the night and fears the day:
All men who do or even imagine ill   15
  Fly me, and from the glory of my ray
Good minds and open actions take new might,
Until diminished by the reign of Night.

IV

I feed the clouds, the rainbows and the flowers
  With their aethereal colours; the moon's globe   20
And the pure stars in their eternal bowers
  Are cinctured with my power as with a robe;
Whatever lamps on Earth or Heaven may shine
Are portions of one power, which is mine.

V

I stand at noon upon the peak of Heaven,   25
  Then with unwilling steps I wander down
Into the clouds of the Atlantic even;
  For grief that I depart they weep and frown:
What look is more delightful than the smile
With which I soothe them from the western isle?   30

VI

I am the eye with which the Universe
  Beholds itself and knows itself divine;
All harmony of instrument or verse,
  All prophecy, all medicine is mine,
All light of art or nature;—to my song   35
Victory and praise in its own right belong.

Hymn of Pan

(Written in 1820 ; published 1824)

I

FROM the forests and highlands
    We come, we come ;
From the river-girt islands,
    Where loud waves are dumb
        Listening to my sweet pipings.   5
The wind in the reeds and the rushes,
    The bees on the bells of thyme,
The birds on the myrtle bushes,
    The cicale above in the lime,
And the lizards below in the grass,   10
Were as silent as ever old Tmolus was,
    Listening to my sweet pipings.

II

Liquid Peneus was flowing,
    And all dark Tempe lay
In Pelion's shadow, outgrowing   15
    The light of the dying day,
        Speeded by my sweet pipings.
The Sileni, and Sylvans, and Fauns,
    And the Nymphs of the woods and the waves,
To the edge of the moist river-lawns,   20
    And the brink of the dewy caves,
And all that did then attend and follow,
Were silent with love, as you now, Apollo,
    With envy of my sweet pipings.

III

I sang of the dancing stars,   25
    I sang of the daedal Earth,
And of Heaven—and the giant wars,
    And Love, and Death, and Birth,—

And then I changed my pipings,—
Singing how down the vale of Maenalus 30
    I pursued a maiden and clasped a reed.
Gods and men, we are all deluded thus!
    It breaks in our bosom and then we bleed:
All wept, as I think both ye now would,
If envy or age had not frozen your blood, 35
    At the sorrow of my sweet pipings.

Ode to Naples

(Composed August 1820; published 1824)

EPODE I a

I STOOD within the City disinterred;
    And heard the autumnal leaves like light footfalls
Of spirits passing through the streets; and heard
    The Mountain's slumberous voice at intervals
        Thrill through those roofless halls; 5
The oracular thunder penetrating shook
    The listening soul in my suspended blood;
I felt that Earth out of her deep heart spoke—
    I felt, but heard not:—through white columns glowed
        The isle-sustaining ocean-flood, 10
A plane of light between two heavens of azure!
    Around me gleamed many a bright sepulchre
Of whose pure beauty, Time, as if his pleasure
Were to spare Death, had never made erasure;
    But every living lineament was clear 15
        As in the sculptor's thought; and there
The wreaths of stony myrtle, ivy, and pine,
    Like winter leaves o'ergrown by moulded snow,
    Seemed only not to move and grow

Because the crystal silence of the air   20
   Weighed on their life; even as the Power divine
   Which then lulled all things, brooded upon mine.

EPODE IIa

   Then gentle winds arose
   With many a mingled close
Of wild Aeolian sound, and mountain-odours keen; 25
    And where the Baian ocean
    Welters with airlike motion,
Within, above, around its bowers of starry green,
  Moving the sea-flowers in those purple caves,
    Even as the ever stormless atmosphere   30
    Floats o'er the Elysian realm,
  It bore me, like an Angel, o'er the waves
   Of sunlight, whose swift pinnace of dewy air
    No storm can overwhelm.
    I sailed, where ever flows   35
    Under the calm Serene
    A spirit of deep emotion
    From the unknown graves
    Of the dead Kings of Melody.
Shadowy Aornos darkened o'er the helm   40
The horizontal aether; Heaven stripped bare
Its depth over Elysium, where the prow
Made the invisible water white as snow;
From that Typhaean mount, Inarime,
There streamed a sunbright vapour, like the standard 45
    Of some aethereal host;
    Whilst from all the coast,
  Louder and louder, gathering round, there wandered
Over the oracular woods and divine sea
Prophesyings which grew articulate—   50
They seize me—I must speak them!—be they fate!

STROPHE I

Naples! thou Heart of men which ever pantest
   Naked, beneath the lidless eye of Heaven!
Elysian City, which to calm enchantest
   The mutinous air and sea! they round thee, even   55
   As sleep round Love, are driven!
Metropolis of a ruined Paradise
   Long lost, late won, and yet but half regained!
Bright Altar of the bloodless sacrifice,
   Which armèd Victory offers up unstained   60
   To Love, the flower-enchained!
Thou which wert once, and then didst cease to be,
Now art, and henceforth ever shalt be, free,
   If Hope, and Truth, and Justice can avail,—
      Hail, hail, all hail!   65

STROPHE II

   Thou youngest giant birth
   Which from the groaning earth
Leap'st, clothed in armour of impenetrable scale!
    Last of the Intercessors!
    Who 'gainst the Crowned Transgressors   70
Pleadest before God's love! Arrayed in Wisdom's mail,
    Wave thy lightning lance in mirth
    Nor let thy high heart fail,
Though from their hundred gates the leagued Oppressors
    With hurried legions move!   75
    Hail, hail, all hail!

ANTISTROPHE I α

What though Cimmerian Anarchs dare blaspheme
   Freedom and thee? thy shield is as a mirror
To make their blind slaves see, and with fierce gleam

To turn his hungry sword upon the wearer;   80
    A new Actaeon's error
Shall theirs have been—devoured by their own hounds!
    Be thou like the imperial Basilisk
Killing thy foe with unapparent wounds!
    Gaze on Oppression, till at that dread risk   85
    Aghast she pass from the Earth's disk:
Fear not, but gaze—for freemen mightier grow,
And slaves more feeble, gazing on their foe:—
    If Hope, and Truth, and Justice may avail,
    Thou shalt be great—All hail !   90

ANTISTROPHE II α

    From Freedom's form divine,
    From Nature's inmost shrine,
Strip every impious gawd, rend Error veil by veil;
    O'er Ruin desolate,
    O'er Falsehood's fallen state,   95
Sit thou sublime, unawed; be the Destroyer pale!
    And equal laws be thine,
    And wingèd words let sail,
Freighted with truth even from the throne of God:
    That wealth, surviving fate,   100
    Be thine.—All hail!

ANTISTROPHE I β

Didst thou not start to hear Spain's thrilling paean
    From land to land re-echoed solemnly,
Till silence became music? From the Aeaean
      To the cold Alps, eternal Italy   105
      Starts to hear thine! The Sea
Which paves the desert streets of Venice laughs
    In light and music; widowed Genoa wan
By moonlight spells ancestral epitaphs,

Murmuring, 'Where is Doria?' fair Milan, 110
  Within whose veins long ran
The viper's palsying venom, lifts her heel
To bruise his head. The signal and the seal
 (If Hope and Truth and Justice can avail)
 Art thou of all these hopes.—O hail! 115

ANTISTROPHE II β

 Florence! beneath the sun,
 Of cities fairest one,
Blushes within her bower for Freedom's expectation:
  From eyes of quenchless hope
  Rome tears the priestly cope, 120
As ruling once by power, so now by admiration,—
  An athlete stripped to run
  From a remoter station
For the high prize lost on Philippi's shore:—
 As then Hope, Truth, and Justice did avail, 125
 So now may Fraud and Wrong! O hail!

EPODE I β

Hear ye the march as of the Earth-born Forms
 Arrayed against the ever-living Gods?
The crash and darkness of a thousand storms
 Bursting their inaccessible abodes 130
  Of crags and thunder-clouds?
See ye the banners blazoned to the day,
 Inwrought with emblems of barbaric pride?
Dissonant threats kill Silence far away,
 The serene Heaven which wraps our Eden wide 135
  With iron light is dyed;
The Anarchs of the North lead forth their legions
 Like Chaos o'er creation, uncreating;

An hundred tribes nourished on strange religions
And lawless slaveries,—down the aëreal regions   140
    Of the white Alps, desolating,
      Famished wolves that bide no waiting,
Blotting the glowing footsteps of old glory,
Trampling our columned cities into dust,
      Their dull and savage lust   145
    On Beauty's corse to sickness satiating—
They come! The fields they tread look black and hoary
With fire—from their red feet the streams run gory!

EPODE II β

    Great Spirit, deepest Love!
    Which rulest and dost move   150
All things which live and are, within the Italian shore;
    Who spreadest Heaven around it,
      Whose woods, rocks, waves, surround it;
Who sittest in thy star, o'er Ocean's western floor;
Spirit of beauty! at whose soft command   155
    The sunbeams and the showers distil its foison
      From the Earth's bosom chill;
Oh, bid those beams be each a blinding brand
    Of lightning! bid those showers be dews of poison!
      Bid the Earth's plenty kill!   160
      Bid thy bright Heaven above,
      Whilst light and darkness bound it,
      Be their tomb who planned
      To make it ours and thine!
    Or, with thine harmonizing ardours fill   165
And raise thy sons, as o'er the prone horizon
Thy lamp feeds every twilight wave with fire—
Be man's high hope and unextinct desire
The instrument to work thy will divine!

Then clouds from sunbeams, antelopes from leopards,
  And frowns and fears from thee,   171
   Would not more swiftly flee
Than Celtic wolves from the Ausonian shepherds.—
Whatever, Spirit, from thy starry shrine
  Thou yieldest or withholdest, oh, let be 175
  This city of thy worship ever free!

The World's Wanderers

(Written 1820; published 1824)

I

TELL me, thou Star, whose wings of light
Speed thee in thy fiery flight,
In what cavern of the night
  Will thy pinions close now?

II

Tell me, Moon, thou pale and gray   5
Pilgrim of Heaven's homeless way,
In what depth of night or day
  Seekest thou repose now?

III

Weary Wind, who wanderest
Like the world's rejected guest,   10
Hast thou still some secret nest
  On the tree or billow?

To Night

(Written 1821; published 1824)

I

SWIFTLY walk o'er the western wave,
  Spirit of Night!
Out of the misty eastern cave,
Where, all the long and lone daylight,

Thou wovest dreams of joy and fear,   5
Which make thee terrible and dear,—
    Swift be thy flight!

II

Wrap thy form in a mantle gray,
    Star-inwrought!
Blind with thine hair the eyes of Day;   10
Kiss her until she be wearied out,
Then wander o'er city, and sea, and land,
Touching all with thine opiate wand—
    Come, long-sought!

III

When I arose and saw the dawn,   15
    I sighed for thee;
When light rode high, and the dew was gone,
And noon lay heavy on flower and tree,
And the weary Day turned to his rest,
Lingering like an unloved guest,   20
    I sighed for thee.

IV

Thy brother Death came, and cried,
    Wouldst thou me?
Thy sweet child Sleep, the filmy-eyed,
Murmured like a noontide bee,   25
Shall I nestle near thy side?
Wouldst thou me?—And I replied,
    No, not thee!

V

Death will come when thou art dead,
    Soon, too soon—   30
Sleep will come when thou art fled;
Of neither would I ask the boon
I ask of thee, belovèd Night—
Swift be thine approaching flight,
    Come soon, soon!   35

Time

(Written 1821; published 1824)

UNFATHOMABLE Sea! whose waves are years,
    Ocean of Time, whose waters of deep woe
Are brackish with the salt of human tears!
    Thou shoreless flood, which in thy ebb and flow
Claspest the limits of mortality,   5
And sick of prey, yet howling on for more,
Vomitest thy wrecks on its inhospitable shore;
    Treacherous in calm, and terrible in storm,
        Who shall put forth on thee,
        Unfathomable Sea?   10

A Lament

(Written 1821; published 1824)

I

O WORLD, O life! O time!
On whose last steps I climb,
    Trembling at that where I had stood before;
When will return the glory of your prime?
        No more—Oh, never more!   5

II

Out of the day and night
A joy has taken flight;
 Fresh spring, and summer, and winter hoar,
Move my faint heart with grief, but with delight
  No more—Oh, never more!   10

To ————

(Written 1821; published 1824)

I

ONE word is too often profaned
 For me to profane it,
One feeling too falsely disdained
 For thee to disdain it;
One hope is too like despair   5
 For prudence to smother,
And pity from thee more dear
 Than that from another.

II

I can give not what men call love,
 But wilt thou accept not   10
The worship the heart lifts above
 And the Heavens reject not,—
The desire of the moth for the star,
 Of the night for the morrow,
The devotion to something afar   15
 From the sphere of our sorrow?

The Boat on the Serchio

(Written 1821; published in part, 1824; in enlarged form in
W. M. Rossetti's edition of the Poetical Works, 1870)

OUR boat is asleep on Serchio's stream,
Its sails are folded like thoughts in a dream,
The helm sways idly, hither and thither;
   Dominic, the boatman, has brought the mast,
   And the oars, and the sails; but 'tis sleeping fast, 5
Like a beast, unconscious of its tether.

The stars burnt out in the pale blue air,
And the thin white moon lay withering there;
To tower, and cavern, and rift, and tree,
The owl and the bat fled drowsily.   10
Day had kindled the dewy woods,
   And the rocks above and the stream below,
And the vapours in their multitudes,
   And the Apennines' shroud of summer snow,
And clothed with light of aëry gold   15
The mist in their eastern caves uprolled.

Day had awakened all things that be,
The lark and the thrush and the swallow free,
   And the milkmaid's song and the mower's scythe,
And the matin-bell and the mountain bee: 20
Fireflies were quenched on the dewy corn,
   Glow-worms went out on the river's brim,
   Like lamps which a student forgets to trim:
The beetle forgot to wind his horn,
   The crickets were still in the meadow and hill: 25
Like a flock of rooks at a farmer's gun
Night's dreams and terrors, every one,
Fled from the brains which are their prey
From the lamp's death to the morning ray.

All rose to do the task He set to each,   30
  Who shaped us to His ends and not our own;
The million rose to learn, and one to teach
  What none yet ever knew or can be known.
    And many rose
  Whose woe was such that fear became desire;—   35
Melchior and Lionel were not among those;
They from the throng of men had stepped aside,
And made their home under the green hill-side.
It was that hill, whose intervening brow
  Screens Lucca from the Pisan's envious eye,   40
Which the circumfluous plain waving below,
  Like a wide lake of green fertility,
With streams and fields and marshes bare,
  Divides from the far Apennines—which lie
Islanded in the immeasurable air.   45

'What think you, as she lies in her green cove,
Our little sleeping boat is dreaming of?'
'If morning dreams are true, why I should guess
That she was dreaming of our idleness,
And of the miles of watery way   50
We should have led her by this time of day.'—

  'Never mind,' said Lionel,
 'Give care to the winds, they can bear it well
About yon poplar-tops; and see
The white clouds are driving merrily,   55
And the stars we miss this morn will light
More willingly our return to-night.—
How it whistles, Dominic's long black hair!
List, my dear fellow; the breeze blows fair:
Hear how it sings into the air—'   60

—'Of us and of our lazy motions,'
    Impatiently said Melchior,
'If I can guess a boat's emotions;
    And how we ought, two hours before,
To have been the devil knows where.'   65
And then, in such transalpine Tuscan
As would have killed a Della-Cruscan,

.   .   .   .

So, Lionel according to his art
  Weaving his idle words, Melchior said:
    'She dreams that we are not yet out of bed;   70
We'll put a soul into her, and a heart
Which like a dove chased by a dove shall beat.'

.   .   .   .

    'Ay, heave the ballast overboard,
  And stow the eatables in the aft locker.'
'Would not this keg be best a little lowered?'   75
'No, now all's right.' 'Those bottles of warm tea—
(Give me some straw)—must be stowed tenderly;
Such as we used, in summer after six,
To cram in greatcoat pockets, and to mix
Hard eggs and radishes and rolls at Eton,   80
And, couched on stolen hay in those green harbours
Farmers called gaps, and we schoolboys called arbours,
Would feast till eight.'

.   .   .   .

    With a bottle in one hand,
As if his very soul were at a stand,   85
Lionel stood—when Melchior brought him steady:—
'Sit at the helm—fasten this sheet—all ready!'

The chain is loosed, the sails are spread,
  The living breath is fresh behind,
As, with dews and sunrise fed,   90

Comes the laughing morning wind;—
The sails are full, the boat makes head
Against the Serchio's torrent fierce,
Then flags with intermitting course,
   And hangs upon the wave, and stems   95
   The tempest of the . . .
Which fervid from its mountain source
Shallow, smooth and strong doth come,—
Swift as fire, tempestuously
It sweeps into the affrighted sea;   100
In morning's smile its eddies coil,
Its billows sparkle, toss and boil,
Torturing all its quiet light
Into columns fierce and bright.

   The Serchio, twisting forth   105
Between the marble barriers which it clove
   At Ripafratta, leads through the dread chasm
The wave that died the death which lovers love,
   Living in what it sought; as if this spasm
Had not yet passed, the toppling mountains cling, 110
   But the clear stream in full enthusiasm
Pours itself on the plain, then wandering
   Down one clear path of effluence crystalline
Sends its superfluous waves, that they may fling
   At Arno's feet tribute of corn and wine;   115
Then, through the pestilential deserts wild
   Of tangled marsh and woods of stunted pine,
It rushes to the Ocean.

When the Lamp is Shattered

(Written 1822; published 1824)

I

WHEN the lamp is shattered
The light in the dust lies dead—
   When the cloud is scattered
The rainbow's glory is shed.
   When the lute is broken,   5
Sweet tones are remembered not;
   When the lips have spoken,
Loved accents are soon forgot.

II

   As music and splendour
Survive not the lamp and the lute,   10
   The heart's echoes render
No song when the spirit is mute:—
   No song but sad dirges,
Like the wind through a ruined cell,
   Or the mournful surges   15
That ring the dead seaman's knell.

III

   When hearts have once mingled
Love first leaves the well-built nest;
   The weak one is singled
To endure what it once possessed.   20
   O Love! who bewailest
The frailty of all things here,
   Why choose you the frailest
For your cradle, your home, and your bier?

IV

Its passions will rock thee   25
As the storms rock the ravens on high;
   Bright reason will mock thee,
Like the sun from a wintry sky.
   From thy nest every rafter
Will rot, and thine eagle home   30
   Leave thee naked to laughter,
When leaves fall and cold winds come.

To Jane: The Invitation

(Written 1822; published, together with *The Recollection*, in one
poem as *The Pine Forest of the Cascine near Pisa* in Posthumous
Poems, 1824; republished separately in present form, 2nd ed., 1839)

BEST and brightest, come away!
Fairer far than this fair Day,
Which, like thee to those in sorrow,
Comes to bid a sweet good-morrow
To the rough Year just awake   5
In its cradle on the brake.
The brightest hour of unborn Spring,
Through the winter wandering,
Found, it seems, the halcyon Morn
To hoar February born.   10
Bending from Heaven, in azure mirth,
It kissed the forehead of the Earth,
And smiled upon the silent sea,
And bade the frozen streams be free,
And waked to music all their fountains,   15
And breathed upon the frozen mountains,
And like a prophetess of May
Strewed flowers upon the barren way,
Making the wintry world appear
Like one on whom thou smilest, dear.   20

Away, away, from men and towns,
To the wild wood and the downs—
To the silent wilderness
Where the soul need not repress
Its music lest it should not find   25
An echo in another's mind,
While the touch of Nature's art
Harmonizes heart to heart.
I leave this notice on my door
For each accustomed visitor:—   30
'I am gone into the fields
To take what this sweet hour yields;—
Reflection, you may come to-morrow,
Sit by the fireside with Sorrow.—
You with the unpaid bill, Despair,—   35
You, tiresome verse-reciter, Care,—
I will pay you in the grave,—
Death will listen to your stave.
Expectation too, be off!
To-day is for itself enough;   40
Hope, in pity mock not Woe
With smiles, nor follow where I go;
Long having lived on thy sweet food,
At length I find one moment's good
After long pain—with all your love,   45
This you never told me of.'

Radiant Sister of the Day,
Awake! arise! and come away!
To the wild woods and the plains,
And the pools where winter rains   50
Image all their roof of leaves,
Where the pine its garland weaves

Of sapless green and ivy dun
Round stems that never kiss the sun;
Where the lawns and pastures be,   55
And the sandhills of the sea;—
Where the melting hoar-frost wets
The daisy-star that never sets,
And wind-flowers, and violets,
Which yet join not scent to hue,   60
Crown the pale year weak and new;
When the night is left behind
In the deep east, dun and blind,
And the blue noon is over us,
And the multitudinous   65
Billows murmur at our feet,
Where the earth and ocean meet,
And all things seem only one
In the universal sun.

With a Guitar, to Jane

(Written 1822; first published in *The Athenæum*, 20 October 1832)

ARIEL to Miranda:—Take
This slave of Music, for the sake
Of him who is the slave of thee,
And teach it all the harmony
In which thou canst, and only thou,   5
Make the delighted spirit glow,
Till joy denies itself again,
And, too intense, is turned to pain;
For by permission and command
Of thine own Prince Ferdinand,   10
Poor Ariel sends this silent token
Of more than ever can be spoken;
Your guardian spirit, Ariel, who,
From life to life, must still pursue

Your happiness;—for thus alone   15
Can Ariel ever find his own.
From Prospero's enchanted cell,
As the mighty verses tell,
To the throne of Naples, he
Lit you o'er the trackless sea,   20
Flitting on, your prow before,
Like a living meteor.
When you die, the silent Moon,
In her interlunar swoon,
Is not sadder in her cell   25
Than deserted Ariel.
When you live again on earth,
Like an unseen star of birth,
Ariel guides you o'er the sea
Of life from your nativity.   30
Many changes have been run
Since Ferdinand and you begun
Your course of love, and Ariel still
Has tracked your steps, and served your will;
Now, in humbler, happier lot,   35
This is all remembered not;
And now, alas! the poor sprite is
Imprisoned, for some fault of his,
In a body like a grave;—
From you he only dares to crave,   40
For his service and his sorrow,
A smile to-day, a song to-morrow.

The artist who this idol wrought,
To echo all harmonious thought,
Felled a tree, while on the steep   45
The woods were in their winter sleep,

Rocked in that repose divine
On the wind-swept Apennine;
And dreaming, some of Autumn past,
And some of Spring approaching fast,   50
And some of April buds and showers,
And some of songs in July bowers,
And all of love; and so this tree,—
O that such our death may be!—
Died in sleep, and felt no pain   55
To live in happier form again;
From which, beneath Heaven's fairest star,
The artist wrought this loved Guitar,
And taught it justly to reply,
To all who question skilfully,   60
In language gentle as thine own;
Whispering in enamoured tone
Sweet oracles of woods and dells,
And summer winds in sylvan cells;
For it had learned all harmonies   65
Of the plains and of the skies,
Of the forests and the mountains,
And the many-voicèd fountains;
The clearest echoes of the hills,
The softest notes of falling rills,   70
The melodies of birds and bees,
The murmuring of summer seas,
And pattering rain, and breathing dew,
And airs of evening; and it knew
That seldom-heard mysterious sound,   75
Which, driven on its diurnal round,
As it floats through boundless day,
Our world enkindles on its way.—
All this it knows, but will not tell
To those who cannot question well   80

The Spirit that inhabits it;
It talks according to the wit
Of its companions; and no more
Is heard than has been felt before,
By those who tempt it to betray   85
These secrets of an elder day:
But, sweetly as its answers will
Flatter hands of perfect skill,
It keeps its highest, holiest tone
For our belovèd Jane alone.   90

A Dirge

(Written in 1822; published 1824)

ROUGH wind, that moanest loud
   Grief too sad for song;
Wild wind, when sullen cloud
   Knells all the night long;
Sad storm, whose tears are vain,   5
Bare woods, whose branches strain,
Deep caves and dreary main,—
   Wail, for the world's wrong!

To Jane: The Keen Stars were Twinkling

(Written 1822; first published in *The Athenæum*, 17 November 1832;
republished 1839)

I

THE keen stars were twinkling,
And the fair moon was rising among them,
   Dear Jane!
The guitar was tinkling,
But the notes were not sweet till you sung them   5
   Again.

II

As the moon's soft splendour
O'er the faint cold starlight of Heaven
    Is thrown,
  So your voice most tender   10
To the strings without soul had then given
    Its own.

III

  The stars will awaken,
Though the moon sleep a full hour later,
    To-night;   15
  No leaf will be shaken
Whilst the dews of your melody scatter
    Delight.

IV

  Though the sound overpowers,
Sing again, with your dear voice revealing   20
    A tone
  Of some world far from ours,
Where music and moonlight and feeling
    Are one.

From *A Defence of Poetry*

(Written February and March 1821 ; first published by Mrs.
Shelley in *Essays and Letters from Abroad*, 1840)

POETRY, in a general sense, may be defined to be 'the
expression of the imagination': and poetry is connate with
the origin of man. Man is an instrument over which a series
of external and internal impressions are driven, like the
alternations of an ever-changing wind over an Aeolian lyre,
which move it by their motion to ever-changing melody.

But there is a principle within the human being, and perhaps within all sentient beings, which acts otherwise than in the lyre, and produces not melody alone, but harmony, by an internal adjustment of the sounds or motions thus excited to the impressions which excite them. It is as if the lyre could accommodate its chords to the motions of that which strikes them, in a determined proportion of sound; even as the musician can accommodate his voice to the sound of the lyre.

In the youth of the world, men dance and sing and imitate natural objects, observing in these actions, as in all others, a certain rhythm or order. And, although all men observe a similar, they observe not the same order, in the motions of the dance, in the melody of the song, in the combinations of language, in the series of their imitations of natural objects. For there is a certain order or rhythm belonging to each of these classes of mimetic representation, from which the hearer and the spectator receive an intenser and purer pleasure than from any other; the sense of an approximation to this order has been called taste by modern writers. Every man in the infancy of art observes an order which approximates more or less closely to that from which this highest delight results: but the diversity is not sufficiently marked, as that its gradations should be sensible, except in those instances where the predominance of this faculty of approximation to the beautiful (for so we may be permitted to name the relation between this highest pleasure and its cause) is very great. Those in whom it exists in excess are poets, in the most universal sense of the word; and the pleasure resulting from the manner in which they express the influence of society or nature upon their own minds, communicates itself to others, and gathers a sort of reduplication from that community.

But poets, or those who imagine and express this in-

destructible order, are not only the authors of language and of music, of the dance, and architecture, and statuary, and painting; they are the institutors of laws, and the founders of civil society, and the inventors of the arts of life, and the teachers, who draw into a certain propinquity with the beautiful and the true that partial apprehension of the agencies of the invisible world which is called religion. Hence all original religions are allegorical, or susceptible of allegory, and, like Janus, have a double face of false and true.
10 Poets, according to the circumstances of the age and nation in which they appeared, were called, in the earlier epochs of the world, legislators, or prophets: a poet essentially comprises and unites both these characters. For he not only beholds intensely the present as it is, and discovers those laws according to which present things ought to be ordered, but he beholds the future in the present, and his thoughts are the germs of the flower and the fruit of latest time. Not that I assert poets to be prophets in the gross sense of the word, or that they can foretell the form as surely as they
20 foreknow the spirit of events: such is the pretence of superstition, which would make poetry an attribute of prophecy, rather than prophecy an attribute of poetry. A poet participates in the eternal, the infinite, and the one; as far as relates to his conceptions, time and place and number are not. The grammatical forms which express the moods of time, and the difference of persons, and the distinction of place, are convertible with respect to the highest poetry without injuring it as poetry; and the choruses of Aeschylus, and the book of *Job*, and Dante's *Paradise*, would afford,
30 more than any other writings, examples of this fact, if the limits of this essay did not forbid citation. The creations of sculpture, painting, and music, are illustrations still more decisive.

Language, colour, form, and religious and civil habits of

action, are all the instruments and materials of poetry;
they may be called poetry by that figure of speech which
considers the effect as a synonym of the cause. But poetry
in a more restricted sense expresses those arrangements of
language, and especially metrical language, which are
created by that imperial faculty whose throne is curtained
within the invisible nature of man. And this springs from
the nature itself of language, which is a more direct representation of the actions and passions of our internal being,
and is susceptible of more various and delicate combinations, 10
than colour, form, or motion, and is more plastic and
obedient to the control of that faculty of which it is the
creation. For language is arbitrarily produced by the
imagination, and has relation to thoughts alone; but all
other materials, instruments, and conditions of art, have
relations among each other which limit and interpose
between conception and expression. The former is as a
mirror which reflects, the latter as a cloud which enfeebles,
the light of which both are mediums of communication.
Hence the fame of sculptors, painters, and musicians, 20
although the intrinsic powers of the great masters of these
arts may yield in no degree to that of those who have
employed language as the hieroglyphic of their thoughts,
has never equalled that of poets in the restricted sense of
the term; as two performers of equal skill will produce
unequal effects from a guitar and a harp.

We have thus circumscribed the word poetry within the
limits of that art which is the most familiar and the most
perfect expression of the faculty itself. It is necessary,
however, to make the circle still narrower, and to determine 30
the distinction between measured and unmeasured language;
for the popular division into prose and verse is inadmissible
in accurate philosophy.

Sounds as well as thoughts have relation both between

each other and towards that which they represent, and a
perception of the order of those relations has always been
found connected with a perception of the order of the
relations of thoughts. Hence the language of poets has ever
affected a certain uniform and harmonious recurrence of
sound, without which it were not poetry, and which is
scarcely less indispensable to the communication of its
influence, than the words themselves, without reference to
that peculiar order. Hence the vanity of translation; it
10 were as wise to cast a violet into a crucible that you might
discover the formal principle of its colour and odour, as seek
to transfuse from one language into another the creations
of a poet. The plant must spring again from its seed, or it
will bear no flower—and this is the burthen of the curse
of Babel.

An observation of the regular mode of the recurrence of
harmony in the language of poetical minds, together with
its relation to music, produced metre, or a certain system of
traditional forms of harmony and language. Yet it is by
20 no means essential that a poet should accommodate his
language to this traditional form, so that the harmony,
which is its spirit, be observed. The practice is indeed
convenient and popular, and to be preferred, especially in
such composition as includes much action: but every great
poet must inevitably innovate upon the example of his
predecessors in the exact structure of his peculiar versifica-
tion. The distinction between poets and prose writers is a
vulgar error. The distinction between philosophers and
poets has been anticipated. Plato was essentially a poet—
30 the truth and splendour of his imagery, and the melody
of his language, are the most intense that it is possible to
conceive. He rejected the measure of the epic, dramatic,
and lyrical forms, because he sought to kindle a harmony
in thoughts divested of shape and action, and he forbore to

invent any regular plan of rhythm which would include, under determinate forms, the varied pauses of his style. Cicero sought to imitate the cadence of his periods, but with little success. Lord Bacon was a poet. His language has a sweet and majestic rhythm, which satisfies the sense, no less than the almost superhuman wisdom of his philosophy satisfies the intellect; it is a strain which distends, and then bursts the circumference of the reader's mind, and pours itself forth together with it into the universal element with which it has perpetual sympathy. All the authors of revolutions in opinion are not only necessarily poets as they are inventors, nor even as their words unveil the permanent analogy of things by images which participate in the life of truth; but as their periods are harmonious and rhythmical, and contain in themselves the elements of verse; being the echo of the eternal music. Nor are those supreme poets who have employed traditional forms of rhythm on account of the form and action of their subjects less capable of perceiving and teaching the truth of things than those who have omitted that form. Shakespeare, Dante, and Milton (to confine ourselves to modern writers) are philosophers of the very loftiest power.

A poem is the very image of life expressed in its eternal truth. There is this difference between a story and a poem, that a story is a catalogue of detached facts, which have no other connexion than time, place, circumstance, cause and effect; the other is the creation of actions according to the unchangeable forms of human nature, as existing in the mind of the Creator, which is itself the image of all other minds. The one is partial, and applies only to a definite period of time, and a certain combination of events which can never again recur; the other is universal, and contains within itself the germ of a relation to whatever motives or actions have place in the possible varieties of human nature.

Time, which destroys the beauty and the use of the story of particular facts, stripped of the poetry which should invest them, augments that of poetry, and for ever develops new and wonderful applications of the eternal truth which it contains. Hence epitomes have been called the moths of just history; they eat out the poetry of it. A story of particular facts is as a mirror which obscures and distorts that which should be beautiful: poetry is a mirror which makes beautiful that which is distorted.

10 The parts of a composition may be poetical, without the composition as a whole being a poem. A single sentence may be considered as a whole, though it may be found in the midst of a series of unassimilated portions: a single word even may be a spark of inextinguishable thought. And thus all the great historians, Herodotus, Plutarch, Livy, were poets; and although the plan of these writers, especially that of Livy, restrained them from developing this faculty in its highest degree, they made copious and ample amends for their subjection, by filling all the interstices of their subjects 20 with living images.

Having determined what is poetry, and who are poets, let us proceed to estimate its effects upon society.

Poetry is ever accompanied with pleasure: all spirits on which it falls open themselves to receive the wisdom which is mingled with its delight. In the infancy of the world, neither poets themselves nor their auditors are fully aware of the excellence of poetry: for it acts in a divine and unapprehended manner, beyond and above consciousness; and it is reserved for future generations to contemplate and 30 measure the mighty cause and effect in all the strength and splendour of their union. Even in modern times, no living poet ever arrived at the fullness of his fame; the jury which sits in judgement upon a poet, belonging as he does to all time, must be composed of his peers: it must be impanelled

by Time from the selectest of the wise of many generations.
A poet is a nightingale, who sits in darkness and sings to
cheer its own solitude with sweet sounds; his auditors are as
men entranced by the melody of an unseen musician, who
feel that they are moved and softened, yet know not whence
or why. The poems of Homer and his contemporaries were
the delight of infant Greece; they were the elements of that
social system which is the column upon which all succeeding
civilization has reposed. Homer embodied the ideal perfection of his age in human character; nor can we doubt that 10
those who read his verses were awakened to an ambition of
becoming like to Achilles, Hector, and Ulysses: the truth
and beauty of friendship, patriotism, and persevering devotion to an object were unveiled to the depths in these
immortal creations: the sentiments of the auditors must have
been refined and enlarged by a sympathy with such great
and lovely impersonations, until from admiring they
imitated, and from imitation they identified themselves
with the objects of their admiration. Nor let it be objected,
that these characters are remote from moral perfection, and 20
that they can by no means be considered as edifying patterns
for general imitation. Every epoch, under names more or
less specious, has deified its peculiar errors; Revenge is the
naked idol of the worship of a semi-barbarous age; and Self-
deceit is the veiled image of unknown evil, before which
luxury and satiety lie prostrate. But a poet considers the
vices of his contemporaries as a temporary dress in which
his creations must be arrayed, and which cover without
concealing the eternal proportions of their beauty. An epic
or dramatic personage is understood to wear them around 30
his soul, as he may the ancient armour or the modern
uniform around his body; whilst it is easy to conceive a dress
more graceful than either. The beauty of the internal nature
cannot be so far concealed by its accidental vesture but

that the spirit of its form shall communicate itself to the very disguise, and indicate the shape it hides from the manner in which it is worn. A majestic form and graceful motions will express themselves through the most barbarous and tasteless costume. Few poets of the highest class have chosen to exhibit the beauty of their conceptions in its naked truth and splendour; and it is doubtful whether the alloy of costume, habit, &c., be not necessary to temper this planetary music for mortal ears.

10 The whole objection, however, of the immorality of poetry rests upon a misconception of the manner in which poetry acts to produce the moral improvement of man. Ethical science arranges the elements which poetry has created, and propounds schemes and proposes examples of civil and domestic life: nor is it for want of admirable doctrines that men hate, and despise, and censure, and deceive, and subjugate one another. But poetry acts in another and diviner manner. It awakens and enlarges the mind itself by rendering it the receptacle of a thousand 20 unapprehended combinations of thought. Poetry lifts the veil from the hidden beauty of the world, and makes familiar objects be as if they were not familiar; it reproduces all that it represents, and the impersonations clothed in its Elysian light stand thenceforward in the minds of those who have once contemplated them as memorials of that gentle and exalted content which extends itself over all thoughts and actions with which it coexists. The great secret of morals is love; or a going out of our own nature, and an identification of ourselves with the beautiful which 30 exists in thought, action, or person, not our own. A man, to be greatly good, must imagine intensely and comprehensively; he must put himself in the place of another and of many others; the pains and pleasures of his species must become his own. The great instrument of moral good is the

imagination; and poetry administers to the effect by acting upon the cause. Poetry enlarges the circumference of the imagination by replenishing it with thoughts of ever new delight, which have the power of attracting and assimilating to their own nature all other thoughts, and which form new intervals and interstices whose void for ever craves fresh food. Poetry strengthens the faculty which is the organ of the moral nature of man, in the same manner as exercise strengthens a limb. A poet therefore would do ill to embody his own conceptions of right and wrong, which are usually those of his place and time, in his poetical creations, which participate in neither. By this assumption of the inferior office of interpreting the effect, in which perhaps after all he might acquit himself but imperfectly, he would resign a glory in a participation in the cause. There was little danger that Homer, or any of the eternal poets, should have so far misunderstood themselves as to have abdicated this throne of their widest dominion. Those in whom the poetical faculty, though great, is less intense, as Euripides, Lucan, Tasso, Spenser, have frequently affected a moral aim, and the effect of their poetry is diminished in exact proportion to the degree in which they compel us to advert to this purpose.

Homer and the cyclic poets were followed at a certain interval by the dramatic and lyrical poets of Athens, who flourished contemporaneously with all that is most perfect in the kindred expressions of the poetical faculty; architecture, painting, music, the dance, sculpture, philosophy, and, we may add, the forms of civil life. For although the scheme of Athenian society was deformed by many imperfections which the poetry existing in chivalry and Christianity has erased from the habits and institutions of modern Europe; yet never at any other period has so much energy, beauty, and virtue been developed; never was blind strength and stubborn form so disciplined and

rendered subject to the will of man, or that will less repug-
nant to the dictates of the beautiful and the true, as during
the century which preceded the death of Socrates. Of no
other epoch in the history of our species have we records and
fragments stamped so visibly with the image of the divinity
in man. But it is poetry alone, in form, in action, or in
language, which has rendered this epoch memorable above
all others, and the storehouse of examples to everlasting
time. For written poetry existed at that epoch simultane-
10 ously with the other arts, and it is an idle inquiry to demand
which gave and which received the light, which all, as from
a common focus, have scattered over the darkest periods of
succeeding time. We know no more of cause and effect than
a constant conjunction of events: poetry is ever found to
co-exist with whatever other arts contribute to the happiness and perfection of man. I appeal to what has already
been established to distinguish between the cause and the
effect.

It was at the period here adverted to that the drama had
20 its birth; and however a succeeding writer may have
equalled or surpassed those few great specimens of the
Athenian drama which have been preserved to us, it is
indisputable that the art itself never was understood or
practised according to the true philosophy of it as at Athens.
For the Athenians employed language, action, music, painting, the dance, and religious institutions, to produce a
common effect in the representation of the highest idealisms
of passion and of power; each division in the art was made
perfect in its kind by artists of the most consummate skill,
30 and was disciplined into a beautiful proportion and unity
one towards the other. On the modern stage a few only
of the elements capable of expressing the image of the poet's
conception are employed at once. We have tragedy without
music and dancing; and music and dancing without the

highest impersonations of which they are the fit accompaniment, and both without religion and solemnity. Religious institution has indeed been usually banished from the stage. Our system of divesting the actor's face of a mask, on which the many expressions appropriated to his dramatic character might be moulded into one permanent and unchanging expression, is favourable only to a partial and inharmonious effect; it is fit for nothing but a monologue, where all the attention may be directed to some great master of ideal mimicry. The modern practice of blending comedy with tragedy, though liable to great abuse in point of practice, is undoubtedly an extension of the dramatic circle; but the comedy should be as in *King Lear*, universal, ideal, and sublime. It is perhaps the intervention of this principle which determines the balance in favour of *King Lear* against the *Oedipus Tyrannus* or the *Agamemnon*, or, if you will, the trilogies with which they are connected; unless the intense power of the choral poetry, especially that of the latter, should be considered as restoring the equilibrium. *King Lear*, if it can sustain this comparison, may be judged to be the most perfect specimen of the dramatic art existing in the world; in spite of the narrow conditions to which the poet was subjected by the ignorance of the philosophy of the drama which has prevailed in modern Europe.

The drama at Athens, or wheresoever else it may have approached to its perfection, ever co-existed with the moral and intellectual greatness of the age. The tragedies of the Athenian poets are as mirrors in which the spectator beholds himself, under a thin disguise of circumstance, stript of all but that ideal perfection and energy which every one feels to be the internal type of all that he loves, admires, and would become. The imagination is enlarged by a sympathy with pains and passions so mighty that they distend in their conception the capacity of that by which they are

conceived; the good affections are strengthened by pity, indignation, terror, and sorrow; and an exalted calm is prolonged from the satiety of this high exercise of them into the tumult of familiar life: even crime is disarmed of half its horror and all its contagion by being represented as the fatal consequence of the unfathomable agencies of nature; error is thus divested of its wilfulness; men can no longer cherish it as the creation of their choice. In a drama of the highest order there is little food for censure or hatred; it
10 teaches rather self-knowledge and self-respect. Neither the eye nor the mind can see itself, unless reflected upon that which it resembles. The drama, so long as it continues to express poetry, is as a prismatic and many-sided mirror, which collects the brightest rays of human nature and divides and reproduces them from the simplicity of these elementary forms, and touches them with majesty and beauty, and multiplies all that it reflects, and endows it with the power of propagating its like wherever it may fall.

But in periods of the decay of social life the drama
20 sympathizes with that decay. Tragedy becomes a cold imitation of the form of the great masterpieces of antiquity, divested of all harmonious accompaniment of the kindred arts, and often the very form misunderstood; or a weak attempt to teach certain doctrines, which the writer considers as moral truths, and which are usually no more than specious flatteries of some gross vice or weakness with which the author, in common with his auditors, are infected. Hence what has been called the classical and domestic drama. Addison's *Cato* is a specimen of the one; and would
30 it were not superfluous to cite examples of the other! To such purposes poetry cannot be made subservient. Poetry is a sword of lightning, even unsheathed, which consumes the scabbard that would contain it. And thus we observe that all dramatic writings of this nature are unimaginative

in a singular degree; they affect sentiment and passion, which, divested of imagination, are other names for caprice and appetite. The period in our own history of the grossest degradation of the drama is the reign of Charles II, when all forms in which poetry had been accustomed to be expressed became hymns to the triumph of kingly power over liberty and virtue. Milton stood alone illuminating an age unworthy of him. At such periods the calculating principle pervades all the forms of dramatic exhibition, and poetry ceases to be expressed upon them. Comedy loses its ideal universality: wit succeeds to humour; we laugh from self-complacency and triumph, instead of pleasure; malignity, sarcasm, and contempt, succeed to sympathetic merriment; we hardly laugh, but we smile. Obscenity, which is ever blasphemy against the divine beauty in life, becomes, from the very veil which it assumes, more active if less disgusting: it is a monster for which the corruption of society for ever brings forth new food, which it devours in secret.

The drama being that form under which a greater number of modes of expression of poetry are susceptible of being combined than any other, the connexion of poetry and social good is more observable in the drama than in whatever other form. And it is indisputable that the highest perfection of human society has ever corresponded with the highest dramatic excellence; and that the corruption or the extinction of the drama, in a nation where it has once flourished, is a mark of a corruption of manners, and an extinction of the energies which sustain the soul of social life. But, as Machiavelli says of political institutions, that life may be preserved and renewed, if men should arise capable of bringing back the drama to its principles. And this is true with respect to poetry in its most extended sense: all language, institution and form require not only to be produced but to be sustained: the office and character of a poet participates in the divine nature as regards providence, no less than as regards creation.

Civil war, the spoils of Asia, and the fatal predominance first of the Macedonian, and then of the Roman arms, were so many symbols of the extinction or suspension of the creative faculty in Greece. The bucolic writers, who found patronage under the lettered tyrants of Sicily and Egypt, were the latest representatives of its most glorious reign. Their poetry is intensely melodious; like the odour of the tuberose, it overcomes and sickens the spirit with excess of sweetness; whilst the poetry of the preceding age was as a meadow-gale of June, which mingles the fragrance of all the flowers of the field, and adds a quickening and harmonizing spirit of its own, which endows the sense with a power of sustaining its extreme delight. The bucolic and erotic delicacy in written poetry is correlative with that softness in statuary, music, and the kindred arts, and even in manners and institutions, which distinguished the epoch to which I now refer. Nor is it the poetical faculty itself, or any misapplication of it, to which this want of harmony is to be imputed. An equal sensibility to the influence of the senses and the affections is to be found in the writings of Homer and Sophocles: the former, especially, has clothed sensual and pathetic images with irresistible attractions. Their superiority over these succeeding writers consists in the presence of those thoughts which belong to the inner faculties of our nature, not in the absence of those which are connected with the external: their incomparable perfection consists in a harmony of the union of all. It is not what the erotic poets have, but what they have not, in which their imperfection consists. It is not inasmuch as they were poets, but inasmuch as they were not poets, that they can be considered with any plausibility as connected with the corruption of their age. Had that corruption availed so as to extinguish in them the sensibility to pleasure, passion, and natural scenery, which is imputed to them as an imperfection, the last triumph of evil would have been achieved. For the end of social corruption is to destroy all sensibility to pleasure; and, therefore, it is corruption. It begins at the imagination and the intellect as at the core, and distributes itself thence as a paralysing venom, through the affections into the very appetites, until all become a torpid mass in which hardly sense survives. At the approach of such a period, poetry ever addresses itself to those faculties which 10 are the last to be destroyed, and its voice is heard, like the footsteps of Astraea, departing from the world. Poetry ever communicates all the pleasure which men are capable of receiving: it is ever still the light of life; the source of whatever of beautiful or generous or true can have place in an evil time. It will readily be confessed that those among the luxurious citizens of Syracuse and Alexandria who were delighted with the poems of Theocritus were less cold, cruel, and sensual than the remnant of their tribe. But corruption must utterly have destroyed the fabric of 20 human society before poetry can ever cease. The sacred links of that chain have never been entirely disjoined, which descending through the minds of many men is attached to those great minds, whence as from a magnet the invisible effluence is sent forth which at once connects, animates, and sustains the life of all. It is the faculty which contains within itself the seeds at once of its own and of social renovation. And let us not circumscribe the effects of the bucolic and erotic poetry within the limits of the sensibility of those to whom it was addressed. They may have per- 30 ceived the beauty of those immortal compositions, simply as fragments and isolated portions: those who are more finely organized, or born in a happier age, may recognize them as episodes to that great poem which all poets, like the co-operating thoughts of one great mind, have built up since the beginning of the world.

The true poetry of Rome lived in its institutions; for whatever of beautiful, true, and majestic they contained, could have sprung only from the faculty which creates the order in which they consist. The life of Camillus, the death of Regulus; the expectation of the senators, in their godlike state, of the victorious Gauls: the refusal of the republic to make peace with Hannibal, after the battle of Cannae, were
10 not the consequences of a refined calculation of the probable personal advantage to result from such a rhythm and order in the shows of life to those who were at once the poets and the actors of these immortal dramas. The imagination beholding the beauty of this order, created it out of itself according to its own idea; the consequence was empire, and the reward everliving fame. These things are not the less poetry *quia carent vate sacro*. They are the episodes of that cyclic poem written by Time upon the memories of men. The Past, like an inspired rhapsodist, fills the theatre of
20 everlasting generations with their harmony.

It was not until the eleventh century that the effects of the poetry of the Christian and chivalric systems began to manifest themselves. The principle of equality had been discovered and applied by Plato in his *Republic*, as the theoretical rule of the mode in which the materials of pleasure and of power, produced by the common skill and labour of human beings, ought to be distributed among them. The limitations of this rule were asserted by him to be determined only by the sensibility of each, or the utility
30 to result to all. Plato, following the doctrines of Timaeus and Pythagoras, taught also a moral and intellectual system of doctrine, comprehending at once the past, the present, and the future condition of man. Jesus Christ divulged the sacred and eternal truths contained in these views to man-

kind, and Christianity, in its abstract purity, became the exoteric expression of the esoteric doctrines of the poetry and wisdom of antiquity. The incorporation of the Celtic nations with the exhausted population of the south impressed upon it the figure of the poetry existing in their mythology and institutions. The result was a sum of the action and reaction of all the causes included in it; for it may be assumed as a maxim that no nation or religion can supersede any other without incorporating into itself a portion of that which it supersedes. The abolition of personal and domestic slavery, and the emancipation of women from a great part of the degrading restraints of antiquity, were among the consequences of these events.

The abolition of personal slavery is the basis of the highest political hope that it can enter into the mind of man to conceive. The freedom of women produced the poetry of sexual love. Love became a religion, the idols of whose worship were ever present. It was as if the statutes of Apollo and the Muses had been endowed with life and motion, and had walked forth among their worshippers; so that earth became peopled by the inhabitants of a diviner world. The familiar appearance and proceedings of life became wonderful and heavenly, and a paradise was created as out of the wrecks of Eden. And as this creation itself is poetry, so its creators were poets; and language was the instrument of their art: 'Galeotto fù il libro, e chi lo scrisse.' The Provençal Trouveurs, or inventors, preceded Petrarch, whose verses are as spells, which unseal the inmost enchanted fountains of the delight which is in the grief of love. It is impossible to feel them without becoming a portion of that beauty which we contemplate: it were superfluous to explain how the gentleness and the elevation of mind connected with these sacred emotions can render men more amiable, more generous and wise, and lift them out

of the dull vapours of the little world of self. Dante understood the secret things of love even more than Petrarch.
His *Vita Nuova* is an inexhaustible fountain of purity of
sentiment and language: it is the idealized history of that
period, and those intervals of his life which were dedicated
to love. His apotheosis of Beatrice in Paradise, and the
gradations of his own love and her loveliness, by which as
by steps he feigns himself to have ascended to the throne
of the Supreme Cause, is the most glorious imagination of
10 modern poetry. The acutest critics have justly reversed the
judgement of the vulgar, and the order of the great acts of
the 'Divine Drama', in the measure of the admiration which
they accord to the Hell, Purgatory, and Paradise. The
latter is a perpetual hymn of everlasting love. Love, which
found a worthy poet in Plato alone of all the ancients, has
been celebrated by a chorus of the greatest writers of the
renovated world; and the music has penetrated the caverns
of society, and its echoes still drown the dissonance of arms
and superstition. At successive intervals, Ariosto, Tasso,
20 Shakespeare, Spenser, Calderon, Rousseau, and the great
writers of our own age, have celebrated the dominion of love,
planting as it were trophies in the human mind of that
sublimest victory over sensuality and force. The true relation borne to each other by the sexes into which human
kind is distributed has become less misunderstood; and if
the error which confounded diversity with inequality of the
powers of the two sexes has been partially recognized in the
opinions and institutions of modern Europe, we owe this
great benefit to the worship of which chivalry was the law,
30 and poets the prophets.

The poetry of Dante may be considered as the bridge
thrown over the stream of time, which unites the modern
and ancient world. The distorted notions of invisible things
which Dante and his rival Milton have idealized are merely

the mask and the mantle in which these great poets walk through eternity enveloped and disguised. It is a difficult question to determine how far they were conscious of the distinction which must have subsisted in their minds between their own creeds and that of the people. Dante at least appears to wish to mark the full extent of it by placing Riphaeus, whom Virgil calls *justissimus unus*, in Paradise, and observing a most heretical caprice in his distribution of rewards and punishments. And Milton's poem contains within itself a philosophical refutation of that system of 10 which, by a strange and natural antithesis, it has been a chief popular support. Nothing can exceed the energy and magnificence of the character of Satan as expressed in *Paradise Lost.* It is a mistake to suppose that he could ever have been intended for the popular personification of evil. Implacable hate, patient cunning, and a sleepless refinement of device to inflict the extremest anguish on an enemy, these things are evil; and, although venial in a slave, are not to be forgiven in a tyrant; although redeemed by much that ennobles his defeat in one subdued, are marked by all that 20 dishonours his conquest in the victor. Milton's Devil as a moral being is as far superior to his God as one who perseveres in some purpose which he has conceived to be excellent in spite of adversity and torture is to one who in the cold security of undoubted triumph inflicts the most horrible revenge upon his enemy, not from any mistaken notion of inducing him to repent of a perseverance in enmity, but with the alleged design of exasperating him to deserve new torments. Milton has so far violated the popular creed (if this shall be judged to be a violation) as to have alleged 30 no superiority of moral virtue to his God over his Devil. And this bold neglect of a direct moral purpose is the most decisive proof of the supremacy of Milton's genius. He mingled as it were the elements of human nature as colours

upon a single pallet, and arranged them in the composition of his great picture according to the laws of epic truth; that is, according to the laws of that principle by which a series of actions of the external universe and of intelligent and ethical beings is calculated to excite the sympathy of succeeding generations of mankind. The *Divina Commedia* and *Paradise Lost* have conferred upon modern mythology a systematic form; and when change and time shall have added one more superstition to the mass of those which have
10 arisen and decayed upon the earth, commentators will be learnedly employed in elucidating the religion of ancestral Europe, only not utterly forgotten because it will have been stamped with the eternity of genius.

Homer was the first and Dante the second epic poet: that is, the second poet, the series of whose creations bore a defined and intelligible relation to the knowledge and sentiment and religion of the age in which he lived, and of the ages which followed it: developing itself in correspondence with their development. For Lucretius had limed the wings
20 of his swift spirit in the dregs of the sensible world; and Virgil, with a modesty that ill became his genius, had affected the fame of an imitator, even whilst he created anew all that he copied; and none among the flock of mock-birds, though their notes were sweet, Apollonius Rhodius, Quintus Calaber, Nonnus, Lucan, Statius, or Claudian, have sought even to fulfil a single condition of epic truth. Milton was the third epic poet. For if the title of epic in its highest sense be refused to the *Aeneid*, still less can it be conceded to the *Orlando Furioso*, the *Gerusalemme Liberata*, the *Lusiad*, or
30 the *Fairy Queen*.

Dante and Milton were both deeply penetrated with the ancient religion of the civilized world; and its spirit exists in their poetry probably in the same proportion as its forms survived in the unreformed worship of modern Europe.

The one preceded and the other followed the Reformation at almost equal intervals. Dante was the first religious reformer, and Luther surpassed him rather in the rudeness and acrimony than in the boldness of his censures of papal usurpation. Dante was the first awakener of entranced Europe; he created a language, in itself music and persuasion, out of chaos of inharmonious barbarisms. He was the congregator of those great spirits who presided over the resurrection of learning; the Lucifer of that starry flock which in the thirteenth century shone forth from republican Italy, as from a heaven, into the darkness of the benighted world. His very words are instinct with spirit; each is as a spark, a burning atom of inextinguishable thought; and many yet lie covered in the ashes of their birth, and pregnant with a lightning which has yet found no conductor. All high poetry is infinite; it is as the first acorn, which contained all oaks potentially. Veil after veil may be undrawn, and the inmost naked beauty of the meaning never exposed. A great poem is a fountain for ever overflowing with the waters of wisdom and delight; and after one person and one age has exhausted all its divine effluence which their peculiar relations enable them to share, another and yet another succeeds, and new relations are ever developed, the source of an unforeseen and an unconceived delight.

It is difficult to define pleasure in its highest sense; the definition involving a number of apparent paradoxes. For, from an inexplicable defect of harmony in the constitution of human nature, the pain of the inferior is frequently connected with the pleasures of the superior portions of our being. Sorrow, terror, anguish, despair itself, are often the chosen expressions of an approximation to the highest good. Our sympathy in tragic fiction depends on this principle; tragedy delights by affording a shadow of the pleasure which exists in pain. This is the source also of the melancholy which is inseparable from the sweetest melody. The pleasure that is in sorrow is sweeter than the pleasure of pleasure itself. And hence the saying, 'It is better to go to the house of mourning, than to the house of mirth.' Not that this highest species of pleasure is necessarily linked with pain. The delight of love and friendship, the ecstasy of the admiration of nature, the joy of the perception and still more of the creation of poetry, is often wholly unalloyed.

The production and assurance of pleasure in this highest
10 sense is true utility. Those who produce and preserve this pleasure are poets or poetical philosophers.

The exertions of Locke, Hume, Gibbon, Voltaire, Rousseau, and their disciples, in favour of oppressed and deluded humanity, are entitled to the gratitude of mankind. Yet it is easy to calculate the degree of moral and intellectual improvement which the world would have exhibited, had they never lived. A little more nonsense would have been talked for a century or two; and perhaps a few more men, women, and children, burnt as heretics. We might not at
20 this moment have been congratulating each other on the abolition of the Inquisition in Spain. But it exceeds all imagination to conceive what would have been the moral condition of the world if neither Dante, Petrarch, Boccaccio, Chaucer, Shakespeare, Calderon, Lord Bacon, nor Milton, had ever existed; if Raphael and Michael Angelo had never been born; if the Hebrew poetry had never been translated; if a revival of the study of Greek literature had never taken place; if no monuments of ancient sculpture had been handed down to us; and if the poetry of the religion of the
30 ancient world had been extinguished together with its belief. The human mind could never, except by the intervention of these excitements, have been awakened to the invention of the grosser sciences, and that application of analytical reasoning to the aberrations of society, which it is now

attempted to exalt over the direct expression of the inventive and creative faculty itself.

We have more moral, political, and historical wisdom than we know how to reduce into practice; we have more scientific and economical knowledge than can be accommodated to the just distribution of the produce which it multiplies. The poetry in these systems of thought is concealed by the accumulation of facts and calculating processes. There is no want of knowledge respecting what is wisest and best in morals, government, and political economy, or at least, what is wiser and better than what men now practise and endure. But we let '*I dare not* wait upon *I would*, like the poor cat in the adage'. We want the creative faculty to imagine that which we know; we want the generous impulse to act that which we imagine; we want the poetry of life: our calculations have outrun conception; we have eaten more than we can digest. The cultivation of those sciences which have enlarged the limits of the empire of man over the external world has, for want of the poetical faculty, proportionally circumscribed those of the internal world; and man, having enslaved the elements, remains himself a slave. To what but a cultivation of the mechanical arts in a degree disproportioned to the presence of the creative faculty, which is the basis of all knowledge, is to be attributed the abuse of all invention for abridging and combining labour, to the exasperation of the inequality of mankind? From what other cause has it arisen that the discoveries which should have lightened have added a weight to the curse imposed on Adam? Poetry, and the principle of Self, of which money is the visible incarnation, are the God and Mammon of the world.

Poetry is indeed something divine. It is at once the centre and circumference of knowledge; it is that which comprehends all science, and that to which all science must

be referred. It is at the same time the root and blossom of all other systems of thought; it is that from which all spring, and that which adorns all; and that which, if blighted, denies the fruit and the seed, and withholds from the barren world the nourishment and the succession of the scions of the tree of life. It is the perfect and consummate surface and bloom of all things; it is as the odour and the colour of the rose to the texture of the elements which compose it, as the form and splendour of unfaded beauty to the secrets of
10 anatomy and corruption. What were virtue, love, patriotism, friendship—what were the scenery of this beautiful universe which we inhabit; what were our consolations on this side of the grave—and what were our aspirations beyond it, if poetry did not ascend to bring light and fire from those eternal regions where the owl-winged faculty of calculation dare not ever soar? Poetry is not like reasoning, a power to be exerted according to the determination of the will. A man cannot say, 'I will compose poetry.' The greatest poet even cannot say it; for the mind in creation is as a fading
20 coal, which some invisible influence, like an inconstant wind, awakens to transitory brightness; this power arises from within, like the colour of a flower which fades and changes as it is developed, and the conscious portions of our natures are unprophetic either of its approach or its departure. Could this influence be durable in its original purity and force, it is impossible to predict the greatness of the results; but when composition begins, inspiration is already on the decline, and the most glorious poetry that has ever been communicated to the world is probably a feeble shadow of
30 the original conceptions of the poet. I appeal to the greatest poets of the present day, whether it is not an error to assert that the finest passages of poetry are produced by labour and study. The toil and the delay recommended by critics can be justly interpreted to mean no more than a careful

observation of the inspired moments, and an artificial connexion of the spaces between their suggestions by the inter-
texture of conventional expressions; a necessity only imposed by the limitedness of the poetical faculty itself;
for Milton conceived the *Paradise Lost* as a whole before he
executed it in portions. We have his own authority also for
the muse having 'dictated' to him the 'unpremeditated
song'. And let this be an answer to those who would allege
the fifty-six various readings of the first line of the *Orlando
Furioso*. Compositions so produced are to poetry what 10
mosaic is to painting. This instinct and intuition of the
poetical faculty is still more observable in the plastic and
pictorial arts; a great statue or picture grows under the
power of the artist as a child in the mother's womb; and the
very mind which directs the hands in formation is incapable
of accounting to itself for the origin, the gradations, or the
media of the process.

Poetry is the record of the best and happiest moments of
the happiest and best minds. We are aware of evanescent
visitations of thought and feeling sometimes associated with 20
place and person, sometimes regarding our own mind alone,
and always arising unforeseen and departing unbidden, but
elevating and delightful beyond all expression: so that even
in the desire and regret they leave there cannot but be
pleasure, participating as it does in the nature of its object.
It is as it were the interpenetration of a diviner nature
through our own; but his footsteps are like those of a wind
over the sea, which the coming calm erases, and whose
traces remain only as on the wrinkled sand which paves it.
These and corresponding conditions of being are experienced 30
principally by those of the most delicate sensibility and the
most enlarged imagination; and the state of mind produced
by them is at war with every base desire. The enthusiasm of
virtue, love, patriotism, and friendship, is essentially linked

with such emotions; and whilst they last, self appears as what it is, an atom to a universe. Poets are not only subject to these experiences as spirits of the most refined organization, but they can colour all that they combine with the evanescent hues of this ethereal world; a word, a trait in the representation of a scene or a passion, will touch the enchanted chord, and reanimate, in those who have ever experienced these emotions, the sleeping, the cold, the buried image of the past. Poetry thus makes immortal all that is best and most beautiful in the world; it arrests the vanishing apparitions which haunt the interlunations of life, and veiling them, or in language or in form, sends them forth among mankind, bearing sweet news of kindred joy to those with whom their sisters abide—abide, because there is no portal of expression from the caverns of the spirit which they inhabit into the universe of things. Poetry redeems from decay the visitations of the divinity in man.

Poetry turns all things to loveliness; it exalts the beauty of that which is most beautiful, and it adds beauty to that which is most deformed; it marries exultation and horror, grief and pleasure, eternity and change; it subdues to union under its light yoke all irreconcilable things. It transmutes all that it touches, and every form moving within the radiance of its presence is changed by wondrous sympathy to an incarnation of the spirit which it breathes: its secret alchemy turns to potable gold the poisonous waters which flow from death through life; it strips the veil of familiarity from the world, and lays bare the naked and sleeping beauty which is the spirit of its forms.

All things exist as they are perceived; at least in relation to the percipient. 'The mind is its own place, and of itself can make a heaven of hell, a hell of heaven.' But poetry defeats the curse which binds us to be subjected to the accident of surrounding impressions. And whether it spreads its own figured curtain, or withdraws life's dark veil from before the scene of things, it equally creates for us a being within our being. It makes us the inhabitants of a world to which the familiar world is a chaos. It reproduces the common universe of which we are portions and percipients, and it purges from our inward sight the film of familiarity which obscures from us the wonder of our being. It compels us to feel that which we perceive, and to imagine that which we know. It creates anew the universe, after it has been annihilated in our minds by the recurrence of 10 impressions blunted by reiteration. It justifies the bold and true words of Tasso: *Non merita nome di creatore, se non Iddio ed il Poeta.*

A poet, as he is the author to others of the highest wisdom, pleasure, virtue and glory, so he ought personally to be the happiest, the best, the wisest, and the most illustrious of men. As to his glory, let time be challenged to declare whether the fame of any other institutor of human life be comparable to that of a poet. That he is the wisest, the happiest, and the best, inasmuch as he is a poet, is equally 20 incontrovertible: the greatest poets have been men of the most spotless virtue, of the most consummate prudence, and, if we look into the anterior of their lives, the most fortunate of men: and the exceptions, as they regard those who possessed the poetic faculty in a high yet inferior degree, will be found on consideration to confine rather than destroy the rule.

In spite of the low-thoughted envy which would undervalue contemporary merit, our own will be a memorable age in intellectual achievements, and we live among such 30 philosophers and poets as surpass beyond comparison any who have appeared since the last national struggle for civil and religious liberty. The most unfailing herald, companion, and follower of the awakening of a great people to work a beneficial change in opinion or institution is poetry. At such periods there is an accumulation of the power of communicating and receiving intense and impassioned conceptions respecting man and nature. The persons in whom this power resides may often, as far as regards many portions of their nature, have little apparent correspondence with that spirit of good of which they are the ministers. But even whilst they deny and abjure, they are yet compelled to serve, the power which is seated on the throne of their own soul. 10 It is impossible to read the compositions of the most celebrated writers of the present day without being startled with the electric life which burns within their words. They measure the circumference and sound the depths of human nature with a comprehensive and all-penetrating spirit, and they are themselves perhaps the most sincerely astonished at its manifestations; for it is less their spirit than the spirit of the age. Poets are the hierophants of an unapprehended inspiration; the mirrors of the gigantic shadows which futurity casts upon the present; the words which express 20 what they understand not; the trumpets which sing to battle, and feel not what they inspire; the influence which is moved not, but moves. Poets are the unacknowledged legislators of the world.

Preface to *Alastor*

THE poem entitled *Alastor* may be considered as allegorical of one of the most interesting situations of the human mind. It represents a youth of uncorrupted feelings and adventurous genius led forth by an imagination inflamed and purified through familiarity with all that is excellent and majestic, 30 to the contemplation of the universe. He drinks deep of the fountains of knowledge, and is still insatiate. The magnificence and beauty of the external world sinks profoundly into the frame of his conceptions, and affords to their modifications a variety not to be exhausted. So long as it is possible for his desires to point towards objects thus infinite and unmeasured, he is joyous, and tranquil, and self-possessed. But the period arrives when these objects cease to suffice. His mind is at length suddenly awakened and thirsts for intercourse with an intelligence similar to itself. He images to himself the Being whom he loves. Conversant with speculations of the sublimest and most perfect natures, the vision in which he embodies his own imaginations unites all of wonderful, or wise, or beautiful which the poet, the philosopher, or the lover could depicture. The intellectual faculties, the imagination, the functions of sense, have their respective requisitions on the sympathy of corresponding powers in other human beings. The Poet is represented as uniting these requisitions, and attaching them to a single image. He seeks in vain for a prototype of his conception. Blasted by his disappointment, he descends to an untimely grave.

The picture is not barren of instruction to actual men. The Poet's self-centred seclusion was avenged by the furies of an irresistible passion pursuing him to speedy ruin. But that Power which strikes the luminaries of the world with sudden darkness and extinction, by awakening them to too exquisite a perception of its influences, dooms to a slow and poisonous decay those meaner spirits that dare to abjure its dominion. Their destiny is more abject and inglorious as their delinquency is more contemptible and pernicious. They who, deluded by no generous error, instigated by no sacred thirst of doubtful knowledge, duped by no illustrious superstition, loving nothing on this earth, and cherishing no hopes beyond, yet keep aloof from sympathies with their kind, rejoicing neither in human joy nor mourning with human grief; these, and such as they, have their apportioned curse.

They languish, because none feel with them their common nature. They are morally dead. They are neither friends, nor lovers, nor fathers, nor citizens of the world, nor bene-factors of their country. Among those who attempt to exist without human sympathy, the pure and tender-hearted perish through the intensity and passion of their search after its communities, when the vacancy of their spirit sud-denly makes itself felt. All else, selfish, blind, and torpid, are those unforeseeing multitudes who constitute, together 10 with their own, the lasting misery and loneliness of the world. Those who love not their fellow-beings live unfruitful lives, and prepare for their old age a miserable grave.

> ' The good die first,
> And those whose hearts are dry as summer dust,
> Burn to the socket ! '

December 14, 1815.

On Love

(Dated 1815 ; published in *The Keepsake*, 1829)

WHAT is love ? Ask him who lives, what is life ? ask him 20 who adores, what is God ?

I know not the internal constitution of other men, nor even thine, whom I now address. I see that in some external attributes they resemble me, but when, misled by that appearance, I have thought to appeal to something in common, and unburthen my inmost soul to them, I have found my language misunderstood, like one in a distant and savage land. The more opportunities they have afforded me for experience, the wider has appeared the interval between us, and to a greater distance have the points of 30 sympathy been withdrawn. With a spirit ill fitted to sustain such proof, trembling and feeble through its tenderness, I have everywhere sought sympathy and have found only repulse and disappointment.

Thou demandest what is love? It is that powerful attraction towards all that we conceive, or fear, or hope beyond ourselves, when we find within our own thoughts the chasm of an insufficient void, and seek to awaken in all things that are a community with what we experience within ourselves. If we reason, we would be understood; if we imagine, we would that the airy children of our brain were born anew within another's; if we feel, we would that another's nerves should vibrate to our own, that the beams of their eyes should kindle at once and mix and melt into our own, that lips of motionless ice should not reply to lips quivering and burning with the heart's best blood. This is Love. This is the bond and the sanction which connects not only man with man, but with everything which exists. We are born into the world, and there is something within us which, from the instant that we live, more and more thirsts after its likeness. It is probably in correspondence with this law that the infant drains milk from the bosom of its mother; this propensity develops itself with the development of our nature. We dimly see within our intellectual nature a miniature as it were of our entire self, yet deprived of all that we condemn or despise, the ideal prototype of everything excellent or lovely that we are capable of conceiving as belonging to the nature of man. Not only the portrait of our external being, but an assemblage of the minutest particles of which our nature is composed; [1] a mirror whose surface reflects only the forms of purity and brightness; a soul within our soul that describes a circle around its proper paradise, which pain, and sorrow, and evil dare not overleap. To this we eagerly refer all sensations, thirsting that they should resemble or correspond with it. The discovery of its antitype; the meeting with an under-

[1] These words are ineffectual and metaphorical. Most words are so—No help!

standing capable of clearly estimating our own; an imagination which should enter into and seize upon the subtle and
delicate peculiarities which we have delighted to cherish and
unfold in secret; with a frame whose nerves, like the chords
of two exquisite lyres, strung to the accompaniment of one
delightful voice, vibrate with the vibrations of our own; and
of a combination of all these in such proportion as the type
within demands; this is the invisible and unattainable point
to which Love tends; and to attain which, it urges forth the
10 powers of man to arrest the faintest shadow of that, without
the possession of which there is no rest nor respite to the
heart over which it rules. Hence in solitude, or in that
deserted state when we are surrounded by human beings,
and yet they sympathize not with us, we love the flowers,
the grass, and the waters, and the sky. In the motion of the
very leaves of spring, in the blue air, there is then found a
secret correspondence with our heart. There is eloquence
in the tongueless wind, and a melody in the flowing brooks
and the rustling of the reeds beside them, which by their
20 inconceivable relation to something within the soul, awaken
the spirits to a dance of breathless rapture, and bring tears
of mysterious tenderness to the eyes, like the enthusiasm of
patriotic success, or the voice of one beloved singing to you
alone. Sterne says that, if he were in a desert, he would love
some cypress. So soon as this want or power is dead, man
becomes the living sepulchre of himself, and what yet survives is the mere husk of what once he was.

To Thomas Love Peacock, from Mont Alègre, near Coligny, Geneva, 12 July 1816

30 THE lake appeared somewhat calmer as we left Meillerie,
sailing close to the banks, whose magnificence augmented
with the turn of every promontory. But we congratulated

ourselves too soon: the wind gradually increased in violence, until it blew tremendously; and, as it came from the remotest extremity of the lake, produced waves of a frightful height, and covered the whole surface with a chaos of foam. One of our boatmen, who was a dreadfully stupid fellow, persisted in holding the sail at a time when the boat was on the point of being driven under water by the hurricane. On discovering his error, he let it entirely go, and the boat for a moment refused to obey the helm; in addition, the rudder was so broken as to render the management of it very difficult; one wave fell in, and then another. My companion, an excellent swimmer, took off his coat, I did the same, and we sat with our arms crossed, every instant expecting to be swamped. The sail was, however, again held, the boat obeyed the helm, and still in imminent peril from the immensity of the waves, we arrived in a few minutes at a sheltered port, in the village of St. Gingoux.

I felt in this near prospect of death a mixture of sensations, among which terror entered, though but subordinately. My feelings would have been less painful had I been alone; but I knew that my companion would have attempted to save me, and I was overcome with humiliation when I thought that his life might have been risked to preserve mine. When we arrived at St. Gingoux, the inhabitants, who stood on the shore, unaccustomed to see a vessel as frail as ours, and fearing to venture at all on such a sea, exchanged looks of wonder and congratulation with our boatmen, who, as well as ourselves, were well pleased to set foot on shore.

The rain detained us two days at Ouchy. We, however, visited Lausanne, and saw Gibbon's house. We were shown the decayed summer-house where he finished his History, and the old acacias on the terrace, from which he saw Mont Blanc, after having written the last sentence. There is something grand and even touching in the regret which he

expresses at the completion of his task. It was conceived
amid the ruins of the Capitol. The sudden departure of his
cherished and accustomed toil must have left him, like the
death of a dear friend, sad and solitary.

My companion gathered some acacia leaves to preserve in
remembrance of him. I refrained from doing so, fearing to
outrage the greater and more sacred name of Rousseau; the
contemplation of whose imperishable creations had left no
vacancy in my heart for mortal things. Gibbon had a cold
10 and unimpassioned spirit. I never felt more inclined to rail
at the prejudices which cling to such a thing than now that
Julie and Clarens, Lausanne and the Roman Empire, compelled me to a contrast between Rousseau and Gibbon.

To Peacock, from Chamouni, 22 and 24 July 1816

FROM Servoz three leagues remain to Chamouni.—Mont
Blanc was before us—the Alps, with their innumerable
glaciers on high all around, closing in the complicated
windings of the single vale—forests inexpressibly beautiful,
but majestic in their beauty—intermingled beech and pine,
and oak, overshadowed our road, or receded, whilst lawns
20 of such verdure as I have never seen before, occupied these
openings, and gradually became darker in their recesses.
Mont Blanc was before us, but it was covered with cloud;
its base, furrowed with dreadful gaps, was seen above.
Pinnacles of snow intolerably bright, part of the chain connected with Mont Blanc, shone through the clouds at
intervals on high. I never knew—I never imagined—what
mountains were before. The immensity of these aerial
summits excited, when they suddenly burst upon the sight,
a sentiment of ecstatic wonder, not unallied to madness.
30 And remember this was all one scene, it all pressed home to
our regard and our imagination. Though it embraced a vast
extent of space, the snowy pyramids which shot into the

bright blue sky seemed to overhang our path; the ravine, clothed with gigantic pines, and black with its depth below, so deep that the very roaring of the untameable Arve, which rolled through it, could not be heard above—all was as much our own, as if we had been the creators of such impressions in the minds of others as now occupied our own. Nature was the poet, whose harmony held our spirits more breathless than that of the divinest.

The verge of a glacier, like that of Bossons, presents the most vivid image of desolation that it is possible to conceive. No one dares to approach it; for the enormous pinnacles of ice which perpetually fall, are perpetually reproduced. The pines of the forest, which bound it at one extremity, are overthrown and shattered, to a wide extent, at its base. There is something inexpressibly dreadful in the aspect of the few branchless trunks which nearest to the ice rifts, still stand in the uprooted soil.

I will not pursue Buffon's sublime but gloomy theory— that this globe which we inhabit will, at some future period, be changed into a mass of frost by the encroachments of the polar ice, and of that produced on the most elevated points of the earth. Do you, who assert the supremacy of Ahriman, imagine him throned among these desolating snows, among these palaces of death and frost, so sculptured in this their terrible magnificence by the adamantine hand of necessity, and that he casts around him, as the first essays of his final usurpation, avalanches, torrents, rocks, and thunders, and above all these deadly glaciers, at once the proof and symbols of his reign;—add to this, the degradation of the human species—who, in these regions, are half deformed or idiotic, and most of whom are deprived of anything that can excite interest or admiration. This is part of the subject more mournful and less sublime; but such as neither the poet nor the philosopher should disdain to regard.

To Peacock, from Bologna, 9 November 1818

WE saw, besides, one picture of Raphael—St. Cecilia:
this is in another and higher style; you forget that it is a
picture as you look at it; and yet it is most unlike any of
those things which we call reality. It is of the inspired and
ideal kind, and seems to have been conceived and executed
in a similar state of feeling to that which produced among
the ancients those perfect specimens of poetry and sculpture
which are the baffling models of succeeding generations.
There is a unity and perfection in it of an incommunicable
10 kind. The central figure, St. Cecilia, seems rapt in such
inspiration as produced her image in the painter's mind;
her deep, dark, eloquent eyes lifted up; her chestnut hair
flung back from her forehead—she holds an organ in her
hands—her countenance, as it were, calmed by the depth of
its passion and rapture, and penetrated throughout with
the warm and radiant light of life. She is listening to the
music of heaven, and, as I imagine, has just ceased to sing,
for the four figures that surround her evidently point, by
their attitudes, towards her; particularly St. John, who,
20 with a tender yet impassioned gesture, bends his countenance towards her, languid with the depth of his emotion.
At her feet lie various instruments of music, broken and
unstrung. Of the colouring I do not speak; it eclipses
Nature, yet it has all her truth and softness.

To Peacock, from Naples, 22 December 1818
Rome

THE Coliseum is unlike any work of human hands I ever
saw before. It is of enormous height and circuit, and the
arches built of massy stones are piled on one another, and
jut into the blue air, shattered into the forms of overhanging

rocks. It has been changed by time into the image of an amphitheatre of rocky hills overgrown by the wild olive, the myrtle, and the fig-tree, and threaded by little paths, which wind among its ruined stairs and immeasurable galleries: the copsewood overshadows you as you wander through its labyrinths, and the wild weeds of this climate of flowers bloom under your feet. The arena is covered with grass, and pierces, like the skirts of a natural plain, the chasms of the broken arches around. But a small part of the exterior circumference remains—it is exquisitely light and beautiful; and the effect of the perfection of its architecture, adorned with ranges of Corinthian pilasters, supporting a bold cornice, is such as to diminish the effect of its greatness. The interior is all ruin. I can scarcely believe that when encrusted with Dorian marble and ornamented by columns of Egyptian granite, its effect could have been so sublime and so impressive as in its present state. It is open to the sky, and it was the clear and sunny weather of the end of November in this climate when we visited it, day after day.

Rome is a city, as it were, of the dead, or rather of those who cannot die, and who survive the puny generations which inhabit and pass over the spot which they have made sacred to eternity. In Rome, at least in the first enthusiasm of your recognition of ancient time, you see nothing of the Italians. The nature of the city assists the delusion, for its vast and antique walls describe a circumference of sixteen miles, and thus the population is thinly scattered over this space, nearly as great as London. Wide wild fields are enclosed within it, and there are grassy lanes and copses winding among the ruins, and a great green hill, lonely and bare, which overhangs the Tiber. The gardens of the modern palaces are like wild woods of cedar, and cypress, and pine, and the neglected walks are overgrown with weeds. The English burying-place is a green slope near the walls, under

the pyramidal tomb of Cestius, and is, I think, the most beautiful and solemn cemetery I ever beheld. To see the sun shining on its bright grass, fresh, when we first visited it, with the autumnal dews, and hear the whispering of the wind among the leaves of the trees which have overgrown the tomb of Cestius, and the soil which is stirring in the sun-warm earth, and to mark the tombs, mostly of women and young people who were buried there, one might, if one were to die, desire the sleep they seem to sleep. Such is the
10 human mind, and so it peoples with its wishes vacancy and oblivion.

To Peacock, from Naples, 26 January 1819

AT the upper end [of the Forum of Pompeii], supported on an elevated platform, stands the temple of Jupiter. Under the colonnade of its portico we sate, and pulled out our oranges, and figs, and bread, and medlars (sorry fare, you will say), and rested to eat. Here was a magnificent spectacle. Above and between the multitudinous shafts of the sun-shining columns was seen the sea, reflecting the purple heaven of noon above it, and supporting, as it were,
20 on its line the dark lofty mountains of Sorrento, of a blue inexpressibly deep, and tinged towards their summits with streaks of new-fallen snow. Between was one small green island. To the right was Capreae, Inarime, Prochyta, and Misenum. Behind was the single summit of Vesuvius, rolling forth volumes of thick white smoke, whose foam-like column was sometimes darted into the clear dark sky, and fell in little streaks along the wind. Between Vesuvius and the nearer mountains, as through a chasm, was seen the main line of the loftiest Apennines, to the east. The day was
30 radiant and warm. Every now and then we heard the subterranean thunder of Vesuvius; its distant deep peals seemed to shake the very air and light of day, which inter-

penetrated our frames, with the sullen and tremendous
sound. This scene was what the Greeks beheld (Pompeii,
you know, was a Greek city). They lived in harmony with
nature; and the interstices of their incomparable columns
were portals, as it were, to admit the spirit of beauty which
animates this glorious universe to visit those whom it
inspired. If such is Pompeii, what was Athens? What
scene was exhibited from the Acropolis, the Parthenon, and
the temples of Hercules, and Theseus, and the Winds? The
islands and the Aegean sea, the mountains of Argolis, and 10
the peaks of Pindus and Olympus, and the darkness of the
Boeotian forests interspersed?

From the Forum we went to another public place: a
triangular portico, half enclosing the ruins of an enormous
temple. It is built on the edge of the hill overlooking the
sea. ⋀That black point is the temple. In the apex of the
triangle stands an altar and a fountain, and before the altar
once stood the statue of the builder of the portico. Return-
ing hence, and following the consular road, we came to the
eastern gate of the city. The walls are of enormous strength, 20
and inclose a space of three miles. On each side of the road
beyond the gate are built the tombs. How unlike ours!
They seem not so much hiding-places for that which must
decay, as voluptuous chambers for immortal spirits. They
are of marble, radiantly white; and two, especially beautiful,
are loaded with exquisite bas-reliefs. On the stucco-wall
that incloses them are little emblematic figures, of a relief
exceedingly low, of dead and dying animals, and little
winged genii, and female forms bending in groups in some
funeral office. The higher reliefs represent, one a nautical 30
subject, and the other a Bacchanalian one. Within the cell
stand the cinerary urns, sometimes one, sometimes more.
It is said that paintings were found within; which are now,
as has been everything movable in Pompeii, removed, and

scattered about in royal museums. These tombs were the most impressive things of all. The wild woods surround them on either side; and along the broad stones of the paved road which divides them, you hear the late leaves of autumn shiver and rustle in the stream of the inconstant wind, as it were, like the step of ghosts. The radiance and magnificence of these dwellings of the dead, the white freshness of the scarcely finished marble, the impassioned or imaginative life of the figures which adorn them, contrast strangely with
10 the simplicity of the houses of those who were living when Vesuvius overwhelmed them.

I have forgotten the amphitheatre, which is of great magnitude, though much inferior to the Coliseum. I now understand why the Greeks were such great poets: and, above all, I can account, it seems to me, for the harmony, the unity, the perfection, the uniform excellence, of all their works of art. They lived in a perpetual commerce with external nature, and nourished themselves upon the spirit of its forms. Their theatres were all open to the mountains
20 and the sky. Their columns, the ideal types of a sacred forest, with its roof of interwoven tracery, admitted the light and wind; the odour and the freshness of the country penetrated the cities. Their temples were mostly upaithric; and the flying clouds, the stars, or the deep sky, were seen above. O, but for that series of wretched wars which terminated in the Roman conquest of the world; but for the Christian religion, which put the finishing stroke on the ancient system; but for those changes that conducted Athens to its ruin—to what an eminence might not humanity have arrived!

To Keats, from Pisa, 27 July 1820

30   I have lately read your 'Endymion' again, and even with a new sense of the treasures of poetry it contains, though treasures poured forth with indistinct profusion. This people

in general will not endure, and that is the cause of the comparatively few copies which have been sold. I feel persuaded
that you are capable of the greatest things, so you but will. . . .
In poetry I have sought to avoid system and mannerism.
I wish those who excel me in genius would pursue the same
plan.[1]

To the Editor of 'The Quarterly Review', from Pisa, ? 1820

SIR,—Should you cast your eye on the signature of this
letter before you read the contents, you might imagine that
they related to a slanderous paper which appeared in your
Review some time since. I never notice anonymous attacks. 10
The wretch who wrote it has doubtless the additional reward
of a consciousness of his motives, besides the thirty guineas
a sheet, or whatever it is that you pay him. Of course you
cannot be answerable for all the writings which you edit,
and *I* certainly bear you no ill-will for having edited the
abuse to which I allude—indeed, I was too much amused
by being compared to Pharaoh, not readily to forgive editor,

[1] *From Keats's Letter written at Hampstead, to Shelley at Pisa,
August* 1820:
I received a copy of 'The Cenci', as from yourself, from Hunt.
There is only one part of it I am judge of—the poetry and dramatic
effect, which by many spirits nowadays is considered the Mammon.
A modern work, it is said, must have a purpose, which may be the God.
An artist must serve Mammon; he must have 'self-concentration'—
selfishness perhaps. You, I am sure, will forgive me for sincerely
remarking that you might curb your magnanimity, and be more of
an artist, and load every rift of your subject with ore. The thought
of such discipline must fall like cold chains upon you, who perhaps
never sat with your wings furled for six months together. And is
this not extraordinary talk for the writer of 'Endymion', whose
mind was like a pack of scattered cards? I am picked up and sorted
to a pip. My imagination is a monastery, and I am its monk. I am
in expectation of 'Prometheus' every day. Could I have my own
wish effected, you would have it still in manuscript or be now putting
an end to the second act.

printer, publisher, stitcher, or any one, except the despicable writer, connected with something so exquisitely entertaining. Seriously speaking, I am not in the habit of permitting myself to be disturbed by what is said or written of me, though, I dare say, I may be condemned sometimes justly enough. But I feel, in respect to the writing in question, that 'I am there sitting, where he durst not soar'.

The case is different with the unfortunate subject of this letter, the author of *Endymion*, to whose feelings and situation I entreat you to allow me to call your attention. I write considerably in the dark; but if it is Mr. Gifford that I am addressing, I am persuaded that in an appeal to his humanity and justice, he will acknowledge the *fas ab hoste doceri*, I am aware that the first duty of a Reviewer is towards the public, and I am willing to confess that the *Endymion* is a poem considerably defective, and that, perhaps, it deserved as much censure as the pages of your *Review* record against it; but, not to mention that there is a certain contemptuousness of phraseology from which it is difficult for a critic to abstain, in the review of *Endymion*, I do not think that the writer has given it its due praise. Surely the poem, with all its faults, is a very remarkable production for a man of Keats's age, and the promise of ultimate excellence is such as has rarely been afforded even by such as have afterwards attained high literary eminence. Look at book ii. line 833, &c., and book iii. line 113 to 120— read down that page, and then again from line 193. I could cite many other passages, to convince you that it deserved milder usage. Why it should have been reviewed at all, excepting for the purpose of bringing its excellences into notice, I cannot conceive, for it was very little read, and there was no danger that it should become a model to the age of that false taste, with which I confess that it is replenished.

But let me not extort anything from your pity. I have just seen a second volume, published by him evidently in careless despair. I have desired my bookseller to send you a copy, and allow me to solicit your especial attention to the fragment of a poem entitled *Hyperion*, the composition of which was checked by the Review in question. The great proportion of this piece is surely in the very highest style of poetry. I speak impartially, for the canons of taste to which Keats has conformed in his other compositions are the very reverse of my own. I leave you to judge for yourself: it would be an insult to you to suppose that from motives however honourable you would lend yourself to a deception of the public.

$$. \qquad . \qquad . \qquad . \qquad .$$

(*This letter was never sent.*)

To Mrs. Shelley, from Ravenna, 9 August 1821

HE [Lord Byron] has read to me one of the unpublished cantos of *Don Juan*, which is astonishingly fine. It sets him not only above, but far above, all the poets of the day—every word is stamped with immortality. I despair of rivalling Lord Byron, as well I may, and there is no other with whom it is worth contending. This canto is in the style, but totally, and sustained with incredible ease and power, like the end of the second canto. There is not a word which the most rigid assertor of the dignity of human nature would desire to be cancelled. It fulfils, in a certain degree, what I have long preached of producing—something wholly new and relative to the age, and yet surpassingly beautiful. It may be vanity, but I think I see the trace of my earnest exhortations to him to create something wholly new. I have spoken to him of Hunt, but not with a direct view of demanding a contribution; and, though I am sure that if asked it would not be refused—yet there is something in me

that makes it impossible. Lord Byron and I are excellent friends, and were I reduced to poverty, or were I a writer who had no claims to a higher station than I possess—or did I possess a higher than I deserve, we should appear in all things as such, and I would freely ask him any favour. Such is not the case. The demon of mistrust and pride lurks between two persons in our situation, poisoning the freedom of our intercourse. This is a tax, and a heavy one, which we must pay for being human. I think the fault is not on my
10 side, nor is it likely, I being the weaker. I hope that in the next world these things will be better managed. What is passing in the heart of another rarely escapes the observation of one who is a strict anatomist of his own.

To Peacock, from Ravenna, August (probably 10th) 1821

I HAVE sent you by the Gisbornes a copy of the *Elegy on Keats*. The subject, I know, will not please you; but the composition of the poetry, and the taste in which it is written, I do not think bad. You and the enlightened public will judge. Lord Byron is in excellent cue both of health and spirits. He has written three more cantos of *Don Juan*.
20 I have yet only heard the fifth, and I think that every word of it is pregnant with immortality. I have not seen his late plays, except *Marino Faliero*, which is very well, but not so transcendently fine as the *Don Juan*. Lord Byron gets up at two. I get up, quite contrary to my usual custom (but one must sleep or die, like Southey's sea-snake in *Kehama*), at twelve. After breakfast, we sit talking till six. From six till eight we gallop through the pine forests which divide Ravenna from the sea; we then come home and dine, and sit up gossiping till six in the morning. I don't suppose this
30 will kill me in a week or fortnight, but I shall not try it

longer. Lord B.'s establishment consists, besides servants, of ten horses, eight enormous dogs, three monkeys, five cats, an eagle, a crow, and a falcon; and all these, except the horses, walk about the house, which every now and then resounds with their unarbitrated quarrels, as if they were the masters of it. Lord B. thinks you wrote a pamphlet signed *John Bull*; he says he knew it by the style resembling *Melincourt*, of which he is a great admirer. I read it, and assured him that it could not possibly be yours. I write nothing, and probably shall write no more. It offends me to see my name classed among those who have no name. If I cannot be something better, I had rather be nothing . . . and the accursed cause to the downfall of which I dedicated what powers I may have had—flourishes like a cedar and covers England with its boughs. My motive was never the infirm desire of fame; and if I should continue an author, I feel that I should desire it. This cup is justly given to one only of an age; indeed, participation would make it worthless: and unfortunate they who seek it and find it not. . . .

After I have sealed my letter, I find that my enumeration of the animals in this Circaean Palace was defective, and that in a material point. I have just met on the grand staircase five peacocks, two guinea-hens, and an Egyptian crane. I wonder who all these animals were before they were changed into these shapes.

To John Gisborne, from Pisa, 10 *April* 1822

I HAVE been reading over and over again *Faust*, and always with sensations which no other composition excites. It deepens the gloom and augments the rapidity of ideas, and would therefore seem to me an unfit study for any person who is a prey to the reproaches of memory, and the delusions of an imagination not to be restrained. And yet the pleasure of sympathizing with emotions known only to few, although they derive their sole charm from despair, and the scorn of the narrow good we can attain in our present state, seems more than to ease the pain which belongs to them. Perhaps all discontent with the *less* (to use a Platonic sophism,) supposes the sense of a just claim to the *greater*, and that we admirers of *Faust* are on the right road to Paradise. Such a supposition is not more absurd, and is certainly less demoniacal, than that of Wordsworth, where he says—

This earth,

10   Which is the world of all of us, and where

      We find our happiness, or not at all.

As if, after sixty years' suffering here, we were to be roasted alive for sixty million more in hell, or charitably annihilated by a *coup de grâce* of the bungler who brought us into existence at first!

Have you read Calderon's *Magico Prodigioso*? I find a striking singularity between *Faust* and this drama, and if I were to acknowledge Coleridge's distinction, should say Goethe was the *greatest* philosopher, and Calderon the 20 *greatest* poet. *Cyprian* evidently furnished the *germ* of *Faust*, as *Faust* may furnish the germ of other poems; although it is as different from it in structure and plan as the acorn from the oak. I have—imagine my presumption—translated several scenes from both, as the basis of a paper for our journal. I am well content with those from Calderon, which in fact gave me very little trouble; but those from *Faust*— I feel how imperfect a representation, even with all the licence I assume to figure to myself how Goethe would have written in English, my words convey. No one but Coleridge 30 is capable of this work.

We have seen here a translation of some scenes, and indeed the most remarkable ones, accompanying those astonishing etchings which have been published in England from a German master. It is not bad—and faithful enough

—but how weak! how incompetent to represent *Faust*!
I have only attempted the scenes omitted in this translation,
and would send you that of the *Walpurgisnacht*, if I thought
Ollier would place the postage to my account. What etchings
those are! I am never satiated with looking at them; and,
I fear, it is the only sort of translation of which *Faust* is
susceptible. I never perfectly understood the Hartz Mountain scene, until I saw the etching; and then, Margaret in the
summer-house with Faust! The artist makes one envy his
happiness that he can sketch such things with calmness, 10
which I only dared look upon once, and which made my
brain swim round only to touch the leaf on the opposite side
of which I knew that it was figured. Whether it is that the
artist has surpassed *Faust*, or that the pencil surpasses
language in some subjects, I know not, or that I am more
affected by a visible image, but the etching certainly
excited me far more than the poem it illustrated. Do you
remember the fifty-fourth letter of the first part of the
Nouvelle Héloïse? Goethe, in a subsequent scene, evidently
had that letter in his mind, and this etching is an idealism 20
of it. So much for the world of shadows!

NOTES

PAGE 1.   BROWNING'S ESSAY ON SHELLEY

First printed in 1852 as the Introduction to a volume of *Letters of Percy Bysshe Shelley*, published by Edward Moxon. All but two of the twenty-five letters were complete forgeries by an adventurer who called himself a son of Lord Byron. Moxon acquired them in all good faith at a public auction, and asked Browning to write the Introduction, which he did, taking the authenticity of the letters for granted. Their spuriousness was presently exposed, and the book suppressed.

BAGEHOT'S ESSAY ON SHELLEY

PAGE 16, l. 24. *Mr. Macaulay*, in his essay on Southey's edition of *The Pilgrim's Progress*.

l. 30. *he himself tells us*, see p. 152.

PAGE 19, l. 30. *In style, said Mr. Wordsworth*, &c. 'Shelley is one of the best *artists* of us all: I mean in workmanship of style.' (Given in conversation with his nephew and biographer.)

PAGE 20.   SWINBURNE'S NOTES ON THE TEXT
OF SHELLEY

The words of Matthew Arnold on the endeavour of Byron and Shelley to give effect in their poetry to ideas may be found in the Essay on Heinrich Heine, *Essays in Criticism*, first series. The comparison between Shelley and Keats occurs in the same book in the Essay on Maurice de Guérin: 'He [Shelley] in general fails to achieve natural magic in his expression; in Mr. Palgrave's charming *Treasury* may be seen a gallery of his failures. But in Keats and Guérin, in whom the faculty of naturalistic interpretation is overpoweringly predominant, the natural magic is perfect; when they speak of the world they speak like Adam naming by divine inspiration the creatures: their expression corresponds with the thing's essential reality.' And he suggests in a footnote the comparison between the *Lines Written among the Euganean Hills* and Keats's *Ode to Autumn*.

PAGE 22, l. 9. *commonwealth of M. Proudhon*, Pierre Joseph (1809–65), a prolific writer on society in a Utopian strain.

PAGE 30.   ALASTOR, OR THE SPIRIT OF SOLITUDE

The Greek word ἀλάστωρ means either an avenging deity, like the Sphinx or the Furies, or the victim of such vengeance. It might have stood here in the latter sense, had Shelley intended it, but he clearly means a persecuting power. Peacock

writes (*Works*, iii. 423.): 'He was at a loss for a title, and I
proposed that which he adopted. . . . The poem treated of
solitude as a spirit of evil.' It would be more correct to say that,
in Shelley's argument, the passion which rejects and requites
the solitary life may be, in a noble nature, ruinous or tragic,
though always the opposite of evil. When the poem was
written the state of his health pointed to an early death. See
his Preface, pp. 155, 156.

l. 23. *I have made my bed*, &c. Hogg (*Life*, chapter II)
represents Shelley, when a boy, designing on one occasion to
get admission to the vaults of Warnham Church, and 'sit there
all night', awaiting developments. See *Hymn to Intellectual
Beauty*, stanza v.

PAGE **33,** l. 109. *Balbec*, or Baalbec, i.e. Heliopolis in Syria,
the seat, in Assyrian times and after, of the worship of the Sun,
now renowned for its ruins.

l. 119. *The Zodiac's brazen mystery*, in the temple of Denderah
in Upper Egypt. On the ceiling of the portico were mythological
figures arranged in zodiacal fashion.

PAGE **36,** l. 198. 'Still' refers to the lute, 'dark and dry' to
the stream, 'unremembered' to the dream.

l. 204. *but one living man*, Ahasuerus, the Wandering Jew.
The legend made him mock at Christ on the way to Golgotha,
and receive sentence to wander over the earth till the Second
Coming.

PAGE **37,** l. 240. '*too deep for tears*',—from the last line of
Wordsworth's *Ode on the Intimations of Immortality*. *Alastor* is
thronged with Wordsworthian echoes.

PAGE **38.**   JULIAN AND MADDALO

This poem recalls the visit paid by Shelley (Julian) to Venice
in August 1818 in order to confer with Byron (Maddalo) on the
disposal of his daughter Allegra, the child of the story, whose
mother was Mary Shelley's step-sister, Claire Clairmont. From
Venice Shelley wrote to Mary at Este that he had ridden
with Byron on the Lido on Sunday, August 23, and the subject
of the conversation was 'his [Byron's] wounded feelings'. The
fourth canto of *Childe Harold* had recently appeared (April),
and its author is in character both in *Julian and Maddalo* and
the Preface to it: 'He is a person of the most consummate
genius, and capable, if he would direct his energies to that end,
of becoming the redeemer of his degraded country. But it is
his weakness to be proud, and he derives from a comparison of
his own extraordinary mind with the dwarfish intellects that
surround him an intense apprehension of the nothingness of

human life. Julian ... is passionately attached to those philosophical notions which assert the power of man over his own
mind. ... Without concealing the evil in the world, he is for
ever speculating how good may be made superior.' In the lines
following this selection, the broken man wanders in the memory
of a slighted love.

PAGE 39, ll. 40–2. See *Paradise Lost*, ii. 559.

PAGE 41, l. 101. *windowless pile*, see footnote to Browning's
Essay on Shelley, p. 9.

PAGE 42, l. 151. *I had nursed* &c. The child was born in
January 1817, and soon after her birth became an inmate of
Shelley's household at Marlow.

PAGE 44, l. 204. '*soul of goodness' in things ill*, Henry V,
IV. i. 4.

PAGE 44.   LINES WRITTEN AMONG THE
                    EUGANEAN HILLS

Written after a day's wandering among the hills about the
villa at Este lent to the Shelleys by Byron in October 1818.

PAGE 47, l. 97. *Amphitrite*, a sea-nymph. See ll. 115 f.

PAGE 48, l. 123. *the slave of slaves*, the Austrian Emperor.
Venice was assigned to him by the Peace of Paris in 1814, and
after the Congress of Vienna was included with his other
Italian possessions in the Kingdom of Lombardy or Lombardy-
Venice.

PAGE 49, l. 152. *Celtic*. Shelley always uses this word when
he should say 'Teutonic'.

l. 174. The Swan is Byron.

l. 180. *sprung From his lips* &c., referring to the Fourth
Canto of *Childe Harold*, written chiefly in Venice, and published
in April 1818, and its concluding lines to the Ocean. Another
judgement is pronounced in a letter to Peacock of December 22,
1818: 'The spirit in which it [*Childe Harold*, IV] is written is,
if insane, the most wicked and mischievous insanity that ever
was given forth. It is a kind of obstinate and self-willed folly
in which he hardens himself.'

PAGE 50, ll. 192, 193. See the above-quoted letter to Peacock
on Byron's manner of life at Venice.

l. 201. *amid yon hills doth burn*, at Arqua, near Este, where
Petrarch often stayed, and where he died.

PAGE 51, ll. 236 f. Ezzelino da Romano (1194–1259), the
head of the Ghibelline faction, and supporter of Frederick II,
was master of Padua and several other cities in Lombardy,
which he governed with historic cruelty. He died after being
defeated and captured by his rebellious subjects in the battle
of Soncino. The main verb of this sentence is wanting.

PAGE **52**, l. 256. The University was still performing its functions at this date, but was closed for political reasons soon after.

PAGE **53**, l. 312. *darkened*, brooded over.

ll. 285–319. These lines from one sentence. The plains, leaves, vines, &c. are interpenetrated by the glory, which is both physical and spiritual, light or odour, love or harmony, soul or mind. It seems best to take 'which' at line 317, as referring to 'soul' (the soul of all things); but the reading 'of all that which falls from heaven'—of all natural and human good—is also possible.

PAGE **55**, ll. 357–70. Their rage would be subdued by the clime and by the winds and leaves; also by the love at l. 366. This interpretation would be assisted by a full stop after l. 369, as in the edition 1839². If a comma is put instead, and 'love circling All things' is taken as nominative absolute, the lines will flow better.

PAGE **56**.   PROMETHEUS UNBOUND

This drama was prompted by the *Prometheus Bound* of Aeschylus and by what is known of the last member of the Aeschylean trilogy, the *Prometheus Unbound*. In the myth there presented the Titan, in defiance of Zeus, befriended the helpless race of men, imparting to them the secret of fire and the arts of life. In requital Zeus chained him to a rock of the Caucasus, and caused an eagle to devour daily his ever-renewed entrails. At last the sufferer bought his release by disclosing to his enemy and man's the impending danger to his throne; for it was fated, as Prometheus alone knew, that, if Zeus should marry the sea-goddess Thetis, he should beget a son stronger than himself. On the disclosure of the secret Thetis was bestowed upon Peleus, and the danger averted.

Shelley could not rest in this lame conclusion. The Prometheus of his drama is an ideal, and also an allegorical figure. He stands for the mind of man and is the lover of Asia, the sea-goddess, who is Love, or the Soul of the World. Jupiter the tyrant is any loveless system, political or religious, that the mind of man inflicts on itself and keeps in power. This Prometheus will not bend, and holds his secret fast; Jupiter marries Thetis, begets a son, Demogorgon, and falls before him. By Thetis, the poet means, in his own word, 'Eternity', the enduring and victorious forces. Demogorgon, the son of Jupiter and Thetis, is, like his mother, that power which determines when a thing has had its day and must perish, and which executes the doom. He is in mythology the Father of the Fates and genius of the earth, who dwelt originally with Chaos, but becoming weary of inaction, arose and formed the earth and heavens; so awful that the Arcadians thought it impious to name him. (He comes in *The Faerie Queene*, I. i. 37, IV. ii. 47; and among the powers of Chaos in *Paradise Lost*, II. 965.) The drama signifies, therefore, that a harsh system of government or belief will try to confirm itself by an alliance with art, thought, and knowledge, and the social instinct (i.e. with Thetis), and will fall by the forces it has used and called out. The rule of Frederick II of Prussia and his successors would be an instance. But this consummation can come only when Prometheus revokes his curse upon the Tyrant, and learning to forgive his enemies, is reunited with Asia. In Act I Prometheus on the rock is tortured by the ministers of the Tyrant who show him spectacles of man's crime and pain; and consoled by friendly spirits, bringing news of men wise and good, e.g. the Poet of ll. 737–51. Before his torture begins, however, Prometheus has revoked the curse, and won his victory. Act II describes the remarriage of Prometheus and Asia; and the 'Voice in the Air' which sings the lyric *Life of Life* (as is clear from a cancelled passage in the so-called MS. B) is that of Prometheus himself, as the influence of love pours upon him. In Act III Jupiter is hurled from heaven by Demogorgon, and the world, human and physical, casts its slough of evil. At the end of Act IV, a long hymn of jubilee from the heavens and the earth, Demogorgon pronounces to the powers of creation the moral rule by which to hold Jupiter thenceforth enthralled (ll. 554–78).

l. 1. *Dæmons*, beings intermediate between Gods and men, as satyrs and fairies.

PAGE 57, l. 25 f. There are echoes of Aeschylus in many of these lines. Cf. *Prometheus Vinctus* 88–92: 'O holy Aether, and swift-winged Winds, and laughter innumerous of sea waves, Earth, mother of us all, and all-viewing cyclic Sun, I call on you.' And cf. l. 44 with *P.V.* 23: 'Welcome to thee shall be night with her garniture of stars when she hides the Sun, and the Sun again when he dispels the morning rime.'

PAGE 60, l. 560. *crag-like agony* &c. Love keeps its desperate hold like a crag clinging to the edge of a precipice, as it were, in agony and terror.

PAGE 61.   LETTER TO MARIA GISBORNE

Maria Gisborne, a woman of great personal charm, and many accomplishments, had moved with her first husband, Willey Reveley, among the friends of the French Revolution in London. She had nursed Mary Shelley after the death of her mother, Mary Wollstonecraft, and had declined an offer of marriage from William Godwin. She was living, when the Shelleys came to Italy, at Leghorn with her second husband, John Gisborne, a retired merchant, and her son Henry Reveley, a civil engineer. In the summer of 1820 she and her family visited England, and the Shelleys had the use of their house, at which this letter was penned in the month of July.

ll. 5–7. Godwin was at this time a bookseller in Skinner Street, and living in neglect and debt.

l. 22. *Shout*, Robert, a statuary.

PAGE **62,** l. 35. *Hogg*, Thomas Jefferson (1792–1862), who was expelled with Shelley from University College, and remained his intimate friend. He was a barrister by profession, and won a permanent place in literary history by his uncompleted *Life of Shelley*, in 1858.

ll. 42–6. *Peacock*, Thomas Love (1788–1866), poet, novelist, and scholar, a close friend of Shelley's, whom he has 'taken off' in the character of Scythrop in *Nightmare Abbey*. He was in the service of the East India Company from 1819 to 1826, and in 1820 married a Miss Gryffydh, known as 'the beauty of Carnarvonshire'. His memoirs of Shelley came out at intervals in *Fraser's Magazine*, from 1858 to 1862. The flamingo, proverbial for shyness, represents Peacock himself, who was rarely seen after his marriage by his former friends.

l. 59. *Horace Smith* (1779–1849), poet, reformer, and stockbroker, joint-author with his brother James of the well-known parodies of contemporary poets, *Rejected Addresses* (1812).

PAGE **63,** l. 81. *yellow-haired Pollonia*, Apollonia Ricci, daughter of the landlord of the Gisbornes' house, murmuring these things to Henry Reveley.

PAGE **64.**   EPIPSYCHIDION

The title is coined on the example of 'epicycle', and means 'a little soul in addition to a soul', or rather 'a soul within a soul', as at l. 126. This is the inmost self of a man which demands perfection in all things, and whose longing after its own antitype in another being is love. This doctrine, which derives from Plato's *Symposium*, is set forth at length in the essay *On Love*.

Shelley towards the close of 1820 made friends with Teresa Emilia Viviani, the daughter of an Italian nobleman, who had sent her, ostensibly for her education, but really for her imprisonment, to the Convent of Sta Anna in Pisa, at the instance of a jealous stepmother. She eventually married the man whom her family forced on her, and died young and unhappy. Until he saw enough of her to be disillusioned, Shelley's ardent sympathy attired her in ideal graces, and she stands in this poem for the 'veiled maiden' of *Alastor* at length encountered. He wished to limit the first anonymous edition to a hundred copies, since 'those who are capable of feeling and judging rightly with respect to so abstruse a composition certainly do not arrive at that number'. In the Advertisement the anonymous writer is said to have died 'at Florence, as he was preparing for a voyage to one of the wildest of the Sporades, which he had bought, and where he had fitted up the ruins of an old building, and where it was his hope to have realized a scheme of life, suited perhaps to that happier and better world of which he is now an inhabitant, but hardly practicable in this'. But while his fable is in this way dissociated from his own person, it remains, as he told Gisborne, 'an idealized history of my life and feelings', and a kind of *Vita Nuova*.

PAGE **64,** ll. 6 f. Shelley here uses the medieval notion of the 'vital spirits', the animating element of the blood, which is not confined to it, but rays out from it, brighter and livelier as the soul is quicker. It is a visible aura, or 'shade', 'made by love', and its 'flowing outlines' mingle with the other glory of the world. At l. 20 'thence' means from the eyes; but the glory is presently said to glow also about her cheeks and fingers.

PAGE **65,** l. 46. *the third sphere*, that of Venus.

PAGE **66,** l. 1. On Aphrodite, Urania and Pandemos, see note to *Adonais*, l. 10.

PAGE **67,** l. 39. *dreary cone of our life's shade*, night being a conical shadow cast by the earth into sunlit space.

PAGE **72.**   ADONAIS

On February 23, 1821, Keats died at Rome of a consumption aggravated by his hopeless love for Fanny Brawne and by the disdain for his poetry among the leaders of popular taste, signally evinced in the reviews of *Endymion* in *Blackwood's Magazine* for August 1818, probably by John Gibson Lockhart, and in the *Quarterly* in the April number of the same year (not issued until September) by John Wilson Croker. Shelley had occasionally met Keats at Leigh Hunt's house in Hampstead in 1817, from February 5 onwards. *The Revolt of Islam* and *Endymion* are said by Medwin to be the outcome of an engagement between the two to write each an epic poem, and they both competed with Leigh Hunt in writing a sonnet on the Nile. In their relations Keats was a little backward, for his pride was shy of a man of birth, and his genius of an impeding influence. Nor was he an admirer of Shelley's poetry; having no will to 'accompany him', as Leigh Hunt says, 'in his daedal rounds with Nature, and his Archimedean endeavours to move the globe with his own hands'. Shelley on the other hand, though he found in *Endymion*, and in Keats's works generally, 'canons of taste the very reverse of my own', saw clearly the promise of his excellence, and in *Hyperion*, in the volume of 1820, the proof. The letter in which, on hearing of Keats's illness in July 1820, he invited him to Pisa (see p. 168), as well as other letters to his friends, and in particular an expostulation written, but never dispatched, to the editor of *The Quarterly* (p. 169) in the autumn of the year, show how intent he was at this time on the present adversity and the prospective fame of one whom he regarded, after *Hyperion*, as 'a rival who will far surpass me'. A second letter of anxious inquiry and urgent invitation was sent from Pisa about February 18th, 1821, and may have come into the hands of the dying man in Rome. Shelley heard of his death about the middle of April, and *Adonais*, 'the least imperfect of my compositions', was finished by the 8th of June. In July it was printed as a small quarto in Pisa, and published in London. In the Preface Shelley states his intention to add in a second edition a critical vindication of Keats as one of the greatest of contemporary poets, and scourges the reviewer of *The Quarterly* in a keen invective.

The Elegy is modelled on the Lament of Aphrodite over the body of Adonis by the pastoral poet Bion, who died about 250 B.C., and the Dirge for Bion by his brother-poet Moschus; particularly on the following passages, of which the verse is from Shelley's own fragmentary translation of Bion, and the prose is Andrew Lang's in *Theocritus, Bion, and Moschus rendered into English Prose* (Macmillan's Golden Treasury Series): The word 'Adonais' is to be taken as a variant of Adonis, not traceable in Greek Literature—it is properly a feminine form—but justified by its music.

FROM THE ELEGY OF BION ON ADONIS

I mourn Adonis dead—loveliest Adonis—
Dead, dead Adonis—and the Loves lament.
Sleep no more, Venus, wrapped in purple woof—
Wake, violet-stolèd queen, and weave the crown
Of death,—'tis Misery calls,—for he is dead.
.   .   .   Aphrodite
With hair unbound is wandering through the woods,
Wildered, ungirt, unsandalled—the thorns pierce
Her hastening feet, and drink her sacred blood.

.   .   .   .

The flowers are withered up with grief.

.   .   .   .
Echo resounds,   .   .   'Adonis dead!'

.   .   .   .
She clasped him, and cried .   . 'Stay, Adonis!
Stay, dearest one, .   .
            And mix my lips with thine!
Wake yet a while, Adonis—oh but once!—
That I may kiss thee now for the last time—
But for as long as one short kiss may live!'

'The flowers flush red for anguish. . . . This kiss will I treasure, even as thyself, Adonis, since, ah ill-fated! thou art fleeing me, . . . while wretched I yet live, being a goddess, and may not follow thee. Persephone, take thou my lover, my lord, for thyself art stronger than I, and all lovely things drift down to thee. . . . For why, ah overbold! didst thou follow the chase, and, being so fair, why wert thou thus over-hardy to fight with beasts? . . . A tear the Paphian sheds for each blood-drop of Adonis, and tears and blood on the earth are turned to flowers. . . . Ah even in death he is beautiful, beautiful in death, as one that hath fallen on sleep. . . . All things have perished in his death, yea all the flowers are faded. . . . He reclines, the delicate Adonis, in his raiment of purple, and around him the Loves are weeping and groaning aloud, clipping their locks for Adonis. And one upon his shafts, another on his bow, is treading, and one hath loosed the sandal of Adonis, and another hath broken his own feathered quiver, and one in a golden vessel bears water, and another laves the wound, and another, from behind him, with his wings is fanning Adonis. . . . Thou must again bewail him, again must weep for him another year. . . . He does not heed them [the Muses]; not that he is loth to hear, but that the Maiden of Hades doth not let him go.'

PAGE 72. FROM THE ELEGY OF MOSCHUS ON BION

'Ye flowers, now in sad clusters breathe yourselves away. Now redden, ye roses, in your sorrow, and now wax red, ye wind-flowers; now, thou hyacinth, whisper the letters on thee graven, and add a deeper ai ai to thy petals: he is dead, the beautiful singer. . . . Ye nightingales that lament among the thick leaves of the trees, tell ye to the Sicilian waters of Arethusa the tidings that Bion the herdsman is dead. . . . Thy sudden doom, O Bion, Apollo himself lamented, and the Satyrs mourned thee, and the Priapi in sable raiment, and the Panes sorrow for thy song, and the Fountain-fairies in the wood made moan, and their tears turned to rivers of waters. And Echo in the rocks laments that thou art silent, and no more she mimics thy voice. And in sorrow for thy fall the trees cast down their fruit, and all the flowers have faded. . . . Nor ever sang so sweet the nightingale on the cliffs, . . . nor so much, by the grey sea-waves, did ever the sea-bird sing, nor so much in the dells of dawn did the bird of Memnon bewail the son of the Morning, fluttering around his tomb, as they lamented for Bion dead. . . . Echo, among the reeds, doth still feed upon thy songs. . . . This, O most musical of rivers, is thy second sorrow,—this Meles, thy new woe. Of old didst thou lose Homer: . . . now again another son thou weepest, and in a new sorrow art thou wasting away. . . . Nor so much did pleasant Lesbos mourn for Alcaeus, nor did the Teian town so greatly bewail her poet, . . . and not for Sappho but still for thee doth Mytilene wail her musical lament. . . . Ah me! when the mallows wither in the garden, and the green parsley, and the curled tendrils of the anise, on a later day they live again, and spring in another year: but we men, we the great and mighty or wise, when once we have died, in hollow earth we sleep, gone down into silence. . . . Poison came, Bion, to thy mouth—thou didst know poison. To such lips as thine did it come, and was not sweetened? What mortal was so cruel that could mix poison for thee, or who could give thee the venom that heard thy voice? Surely he had no music in his soul. . . . But justice hath overtaken them all.'

PAGE **72,** l. 5. *obscure compeers*, not 'selected', like the hour that saw and mourned the death.

PAGE **73,** l. 10. *mighty Mother*, Aphrodite Urania, 'who represents spiritual and intellectual aspiration, the love of abstract beauty, the divine element in poesy or art' (Rossetti); distinguished in Plato's *Symposium* from Aphrodite Pandemos, the 'common' or carnal. There is, no doubt, at the same time a suggestion of the Urania invoked by Milton in the opening of *Paradise Lost*, VII, 'Sister of Wisdom and mistress of Celestial Song'. She is for this reason the 'most musical of mourners' (l. 28).

l. 28. *weep again*, for the next great loss after Milton.

l. 36. *the third*. Cf. *Defence of Poetry*: 'Homer was the first, and Dante the second epic poet, that is the second poet the series of whose creations bore a defined and intelligible relation to the knowledge and sentiment and religion of the age in which he lived and of the age which followed it.'

PAGE **74,** l. 39. *happier they* &c., minor poets content with minor powers.

l. 47. *widowhood*, the barren period since the death of Milton.

l. 58. *Come away!* addressed to imagined mourners in the chamber of death.

PAGE 75, l. 71. *till darkness* &c., i.e. till the darkness of the grave and the law of dissolution cover his sleep not with the semblance of life, but with corruption.

l. 80. *sweet pain,* the bitter-sweet of love.

PAGE 76, ll. 100–8. The splendour is another luminous dream. It was wont to draw strength from Keats's own song, and passing his (Keats's) critical understanding, inspire his heart But now, at the touch of death, it lighted up the body a moment, and was quenched. 'Clips' = 'embraces'.

ll. 114, 115. *led by the gleam,* &c. See note on *Epipsychidion,* ll. 6 f.

PAGE 77, l. 121. *her hair,* streaks of clouds that do not yet drop rain.

ll. 132–4. Echo loved Narcissus, who loved only his own beautiful face, so that she 'pined into a shadow of all sounds'.

ll. 140–2. Apollo loved Hyacinthus, but accidentally killed him with a quoit which the jealous Zephyras directed to his head. Apollo then changed his blood into the hyacinth, marked with the sign Ai Ai ('alas!'). Narcissus pined away for his own face mirrored in streams. Adonais is dearer to the hyacinth and the narcissus than Hyacinthus to Apollo and Narcissus to himself.

PAGE 79, l. 186. *who lends what life must borrow,* i.e. Life must sue to Death for a few years, as a borrower for a loan, and Death soon calls the lending in.

l. 195. *their sister's song,* the 'lost Echo' of l. 127.

PAGE 81, l. 238. *the unpastured dragon,* the unimaginative, the obscurantist, the tyrant, of all whom the poet is the born enemy.

l. 240. The shield of blinding splendour and the spear that quelled at a touch come from Ariosto, *Orlando Furioso,* 55.

l. 250. The allusion is to Byron's castigation of his critics in *English Bards and Scotch Reviewers* and the tribute paid in all the reviews to his next poem, *Childe Harold.*

PAGE 82, l. 276. Actaeon, because he saw Artemis at the bath, was turned into a stag and torn to pieces by his own hounds.

PAGE 83, l. 289. The pansy (pensée) stands for thought or memory, the violet for past sweetness.

ll. 301–2. *an unknown land,* the ideal world ; *new sorrow,* the most recent of his sorrows.

PAGE 84, ll. 307 f. The reference is to Leigh Hunt.

PAGE 86, l. 362. *Thou young Dawn,* see ll. 120–1.

PAGE **87**, ll. 392–6. Life is the degrading power, with its 'low-thoughted cares'. When it contends with the elevating love, the dead live again in their ennobling influences.

l. 404. Lucan was condemned under Nero in A.D. 65, in his 26th year, for his part in Piso's conspiracy, although he had turned informer. He died calmly, after opening his veins and repeating some lines of his own on the death of a wounded soldier. *approved*, i.e. his reputation redeemed, or the spirit that came short in his poetry prevailing in his death, Lucan being called in the *Defence of Poetry* 'a mock-bird'.

PAGE **88**, ll. 415–23. Whoever mourns for Adonais has not felt the might of the 'panting' or aspiring soul which, though imprisoned in the tiny body, can measure the universe. Let his mind measure it, and so discover its own grandeur, lest his heart sink when, after long hope, he arrives at the brink of death.

ll. 424–32. It is no honour to him to be buried in Rome. Rome borrows the honour which he lends.

l. 439. *slope of green access*, &c. Keats was buried, as Shelley writes in his Preface, 'in the romantic and lonely cemetery of the Protestants, under the pyramid which is the tomb of Cestius, and the massy walls and towers, now mouldering and desolate, which formed the circuit of ancient Rome. The cemetery is an open space among the ruins, covered in winter with violets and daisies. It might make one in love with death, to think that one should be buried in so sweet a place.' See his description of it in a letter to Peacock, p. 165. Shelley's own ashes lie here, and his child William was buried here in June 1819.

PAGE **89**, l. 453. *the seal is set*, &c. Shelley's grief for his own child is stilled or sealed.

PAGE **91**.   ODES FROM HELLAS

The Greeks rose against their Turkish rulers, and declared their independence in the spring of 1821. *Hellas*, a dramatic representation of the early course of the war, and a prophecy of Hellenic freedom, on the model of the *Persae* of Aeschylus, was written at Pisa in the autumn. The chorus consists of captive Greek women at the Sultan's court.

i

l. 5. *But they*, &c., the generations of men, incarnating the Mind that ever so passes from birth to death and from death to life again. Properly speaking, not the generations are immortal, but their succession and the Mind in them.

l. 9. *dust and light*, turmoil and splendour.

ll. 11–14. Each generation is glorious or not according to the quality of the institutions and beliefs which it inherits, outgrows, and leaves with the dead.

PAGE 92.

This Ode is sung upon the rumour that Russia and the Western Powers have consented to stand aside, and in the faith that Liberty, if defeated in Greece, will take refuge in the 'kingless continents' of America, and there transcend its ancient glories.

PAGE 93, ll. 19–24. The meaning is: It will be a vain endeavour to revive the Greek legends in our poetry, if Earth is subject to violence and wrong, or in a word Death—a scroll for Death to write on, and if the spirit of beauty in those old stories cannot prevail upon men. It would then be useless to retell the tale of Troy, or cast in some new and subtler version the legend of Oedipus, son of Laius, and the joy of liberated Thebes dashed by the rage of her deliverer. The Sphinx ravaged the land of Thebes, and would not desist till some one from the city should guess her riddle. Oedipus guessed it, and the Sphinx destroyed herself. This Oedipus was the son of Laius, the Theban King, who, being forewarned by an oracle that his son would kill him, caused him to be cast away after birth on Mount Cithaeron. The child was, however, saved by a Corinthian herdsman, and adopted by Polybus, King of Corinth. Arrived at manhood, Oedipus learnt at Delphi that he was fated to kill his father (whom he supposed to be Polybus) and marry his mother, and resolving to flee to Thebes to avoid that fate, met Laius on the road, and in the course of a quarrel slew him, in ignorance of his name and station. After coming to Thebes, and delivering the city, he was made king, and married his mother, Jocasta. The *Oedipus Tyrannus* of Sophocles tells how he discovered his calamity, and having blinded himself in his rage, left the land of Thebes, a voluntary exile.

ll. 31–4. Shelley's own note runs: 'Saturn and Love were among the deities of a real or imaginary state of innocence and happiness. *All* those *who fell*, or the Gods of Greece, Asia, and Egypt; the *One who rose*, or Jesus Christ . . . ; and *the many unsubdued*, or the monstrous objects of the idolatry of China, India, the Antarctic islands, and the native tribes of America.'

PAGE 94.   OZYMANDIAS

Diodorus Siculus, in his account of the history of Egypt. (I ch. 47), describes a funerary temple of Osymandyas (μνῆμα Ὀσυμανδύου) with this inscription: Βασιλεὺς βασιλέων Ὀσυμανδύας εἰμί· εἰ δέ τις εἰδέναι βούλεται πηλίκος εἰμὶ καὶ ποῦ κεῖμαι, νικάτω τι τῶν ἐμῶν ἔργων.

('I am Osymandyas, king of kings; if any one wishes to know how great I am and the place where kings like me lie, let him surpass any of my works.') Shelley knew that this temple had been identified with that of King Rameses II, for whom Osymandyas was the Greek name (formed from his by-name Vasimare). The shattered trunk of the colossus of Rameses still lies among the ruins of the Ramesseum at Thebes. The inscription given to Diodorus by a priest or dragoman is not in the style of the Egyptian kings, and not upon the Colossus, which bears the two names of Rameses II, each followed by 'Sun of Kings'.

l. 8. *mocked*, imitated. So in the *Ode to Liberty*, 'In forms that mock the eternal dead'.

PAGE 94.   To THE NILE

This is the sonnet written to compete with Keats and Leigh Hunt, writing on the same subject.

PAGE 98.   ODE TO A SKYLARK

'It was on a beautiful summer evening, while wandering in the lanes [near Leghorn] whose myrtle hedges were the bowers of the fireflies, that we heard the carolling of the skylark which inspired one of the most beautiful of his poems.' Mrs. Shelley's note, 1839.

PAGE 104.   HYMN OF APOLLO

This and the following 'hymn' were written in 1820 for insertion in Mary Shelley's drama *Midas* (ed. A. H. Koszul, Clarendon Press, 1922). In the opening scene, Apollo, playing on his lyre, and Pan, on his syrinx or pipe, sing each the song here assigned him before Tmolus, the god of the Lydian mountain of that name, and Midas. Tmolus declares that Apollo has won, but Midas favours Pan.

PAGE 106.   HYMN OF PAN

l. 2. He is attended in the drama by the Fauns.

PAGE 107, l. 30. *Maenalus*, a mountain in Arcadia, where Pan was an indigenous god, as much renowned for beauty as the vale of Tempe and its river Peneus in Thessaly.

l. 34. *both ye*, Apollo, who is envious, and Tmolus, who is old.

ODE TO NAPLES

The revolt in the Kingdom of Naples against the absolute government of the Bourbon King Ferdinand, the first effort of

Italian liberalism after the European peace, broke out on July 2, 1820, and accomplished its purpose in a few days. The King, surrounded in his palace, and deserted by his troops, swore fidelity to a constitution. From the first, however, the threat of Austrian intervention hung over the movement. Early in February 1821 an Austrian army crossed the Po, and after one battle entered the city on March 23, with Ferdinand in its wake; and the Constitution was withdrawn. This Ode was written between 17 and 25 August 1820.

l. 1. *the City disinterred*, Pompeii. See letter to Peacock, p. 166.

PAGE **108**, ll. 32–4. *It bore me*, the Baian Ocean.

ll. 35–42. The 'spirit of deep emotion' is that with which the souls of Homer and Virgil brood over the scene. Aornos is the promontory between Cumae and Puteoli, close to which lies Lake Avernus (ἡ Ἄορνος λίμνη). Near the lake was the cave of the Cumaean Sibyl, through which Aeneas, in Book VI of the *Aeneid*, descended to the Nether World and the Elysian Fields. Odysseus, in Book XI of the *Odyssey*, converses with the dead in the land of the Cimmerians, which Homer put on the shores of the Ocean, but later tradition in the forest round the Lake. Homer's Elysium, however, is near the Western Ocean, and no part of the under-world.

l. 44. *Inarime*, also called Aenaria and Pithecusa, i.e. Ischia, a volcanic island in the Bay of Naples, under which the poets fabled that the giant Typhon or Typhoeus was confined by the gods. Homer says he was concealed among the Arimi (εἰν Ἀρίμοις).

PAGE **109**, l. 57. *a ruined Paradise*, the Kingdom of Naples, or Kingdom of the Two Sicilies, or all of Italy south of the Papal States, with Sicily. It was 'half regained' until the Austrian danger should be quelled.

l. 59. *bloodless sacrifice*, the revolution, in Naples at least, had been bloodless.

l. 78. *shield is as a mirror*. In Ariosto and Spenser (*Faerie Queene*, I. vii. 33) it blinds the enemy.

PAGE **110**, l. 81. See note to *Adonais*, l. 276.

l. 83. In medieval fable the basilisk, or 'little king', is lord of all venomous creatures; it has a crown-like formation on its head, and kills with a glance.

l. 100. *surviving fate*, secure against its changes.

l. 102. In March 1820 Ferdinand of Spain was forced by the popular will to call the Cortes, and the Inquisition was abolished.

l. 104. *the Aeaean*, the isle of Aeaea, in the straits between Italy and Sicily.

l. 108. *widowed*, desolated. The Republic of Genoa, after being incorporated in France, was restored in 1814, but at the Congress of Vienna united, as a duchy, with the Kingdom of Sardinia.

PAGE 111, l. 110. *Doria*, Andrea (1468–1560), the greatest of Italian Admirals, who liberated Genoa from the French, and ruled her for many years as the Head of a Republic.

ll. 110–13. 'The viper was the armorial device of the Visconti, tyrants of Milan' (Shelley's note). The Duchy of Milan was ceded to Austria at the Congress of Vienna, and with the former Republic of Venice constituted the kingdom of Lombardy or Lombardy-Venice.

l. 116. Florence, with all Tuscany, was restored in 1815 to the Grand Duke Ferdinand III, brother of the Emperor Francis II, and in that way linked with the Austrian interest.

l. 120. The Pope's sovereignty over central Italy was confirmed by the European Settlement.

l. 123. *From a remoter station*, farther from the goal now than then.

PAGE 112, l. 139. *nourished on strange religions*, the forms of Christianity, which were all, in Shelley's eyes, debasements of the Christian principle; 'strange', therefore, to the 'Heart of men' (l. 52).

l. 161. *thy bright Heaven*, i.e. let them perish under the Italian sky.

PAGE 113, l. 173. *Celtic*, Shelley's usual mistake for 'Teutonic'.

PAGE 117.   THE BOAT ON THE SERCHIO

The Serchio flows through the mountain valley of Garfagnana into the plain of Lucca, and falls into the sea north of the Arno. This fragment recalls a day in July 1821, when the Shelleys were living at the Baths of San Giuliano under the wooded hills that skirt the Pisan plain, and their recently made friends, Edward Williams, an army officer on half pay, and Jane his wife, were four miles away at Pugnano. A canal runs from the Serchio near Lucca to the Arno at the foot of the hills and past Pugnano and the Baths; and by this waterway the families communicated, and might enter either of the rivers, in a small boat which Shelley had previously procured at Pisa. Williams's second Christian name Elleker may have suggested 'Melchior'.

PAGE 118, l. 32. *one to teach*, the poet, who teaches only by intimations, and to whom his own burden is a mystery. Cf. *A Defence of Poetry*: 'Poets are the hierophants of an unapprehended inspiration; the words which express what they understand not.'

NOTES 193

ll. 39, 40. The Monte di San Giuliano. The lines are translated from the *Inferno*, xxxiii. 29, 30.

PAGE **119,** l. 67. *Della-Cruscan*. The Academia della Crusca was founded at Florence in 1582 principally to set a standard of Italian speech. 'Crusca' means the bran that is sifted from the flour.

PAGE **120,** ll. 114, 115. The canal.

l. 116. *pestilential deserts*, the Maremma, or fringe of swamps skirting the sea for many leagues in this part of Italy.

PAGE **122.**   TO JANE: THE INVITATION

This piece and two of the following belong to a group of poems addressed to Jane Williams (on whom see note to *The Boat on the Serchio*) at Pisa in the early part of 1822. Shelley once wrote of her as 'the exact anti-type of the lady I described in *The Sensitive Plant*'.

PAGE **128.**   A DEFENCE OF POETRY

At the close of 1820 Thomas Love Peacock contributed to the single number of *Ollier's Literary Miscellany* a boisterous and half-serious essay entitled *The Four Ages of Poetry*, to the following effect:

(a) Poetry arises in rude societies, where the King, in order to crown his power with his fame, employs a bard to sing of his prowess. The early language being flexible, the numbers flow easily, and in a superstitious age the King is readily provided with a divine ancestry. The poet is nevertheless in these times the only man of mind, the depositary of all knowledge, theologian, moralist, legislator, and often regarded as a portion or emanation of divinity. This is the Iron Age. (b) The Golden Age is that of a Homer, a Pindar, or Alcaeus, an Aeschylus or Sophocles, and comes with the advent of culture. The men of this time refer the marvellous to the past rather than the present, and the poet praises the hero by praising his ancestors. Poetry is now most acceptable, not only because the society is interested in its past, but because the poet presents to it its own strong and passionate characters in artistic forms, and has, as yet, the whole field of intellect to himself, unimperilled by writers or artists of other kinds. But his supremacy is soon threatened by the beginnings of science, history, and philosophic thought. (c) Follows the Silver Age—an age of advanced civilization—which either recasts and polishes the poetry of the Golden or, in its original effort, is comic, didactic, or satiric; the epoch of Virgil, of Aristophanes and Menander, of Horace and Juvenal. The language being now rigid, the poet has much

2179·25   O

labour and scant success, and all the while prose and reason are disabling him. The best he can offer—good sense and elegant learning in smooth numbers—soon tires and palls. (*d*) Poetry, therefore, strikes into new paths in the Age of Brass, and reverts to the barbarism of the Age of Iron, while professing, as in the work of the Greek poet Nonnus, to recover the years of Gold.

The scheme is then applied to English poetry. The Iron Age is that of the medieval romances; the Golden that of Shakespeare; the Silver that from Dryden to Gray; the Brass that of Wordsworth and his peers. Wordsworth and the others have mixed the modern sentimentality into the 'misrepresented ruggedness' of Lake villagers, Scottish cattle-thieves, or the desperadoes of the Near East, and the expansion of truth is fatal to this 'compound of frippery and barbarism', as it is, indeed, to poetry in itself. Poetry is the rattle of an infant society, and the rational and mature will no more use it than rub their gums with coral. As 'the great and permanent interests of human society become more and more the mainspring of intellectual pursuit', men will abandon these 'frivolous studies' for 'useful art and science' and 'moral and political knowledge', and disdain the rhymesters and critics who talk as if poetry 'were still what it was in the Homeric age, and as if there were no such things in existence as mathematicians, astronomers, chemists, moralists, metaphysicians, historians, and political economists. . .'

A Defence of Poetry was written in reply to this article. Shelley received the magazine containing it by 15 February 1821, and on 20 March sent Ollier the first part of his reply for insertion in the second number of the *Miscellany*, which never appeared. He intended to follow up the first part with two more, of which we know only that the second would have applied the argument of the first to contemporary poetry, and defended the practice of 'idealising the modern form of manners and opinions'. The manuscript was transferred after its author's death to the Hunts, who were editing *The Liberal*, which ceased in 1823. With a view to printing the Essay in *The Liberal*, John Hunt, by cancelling a number of references to *The Four Ages*, converted it from a controversial rejoinder to a general discourse on poetry, and in that form it was first published in 1840 and is used in these selections. (Professor A. H. Koszul produced the original draft in *Shelley's Prose in the Bodleian Manuscripts*, 1910.) It is nevertheless plain that Shelley has *The Four Ages* all the time in view. Peacock had argued from distinctions between poetry and prose and between poetry and truth or thought. Shelley, with some aid from Plato's *Ion* and *Sym*-

posium and from Sir Philip Sidney's *Apologie for Poetrie*, elaborates a theory which at once traverses these distinctions, and makes the poetic art the sign and seal of man's well-being.

PAGE **131**, l. 14. *but all other materials*, &c. The 'relations' between the chisel and the stone, for instance, impede the expression. It is strange that Shelley does not consider the claim of music to be the 'purest' of the arts.

l. 34. *Sounds as well as thoughts*, &c. Sounds have a tonic, and thoughts a logical relation to each other; and sounds are related to thoughts (and emotions), as these are to reality. Reality in the poet's vision or thought takes on an ideal harmony. His perception of the ordered relations of sounds to each other (i.e. his musical sense) is always connected with his perception of the harmony created in his thought.

PAGE **133**, l. 7. *it is a strain*, &c.—i.e. it rises into the 'universal element' of Beauty, Beauty being one in essence, whatever its form. It bursts the compass of the reader's ordinary mind, and carries it into that element.

l. 12. *the permanent analogy of things*, the analogy between material and spiritual beauty.

PAGE **137,** l. 20. *a moral aim*, i.e. enjoining a particular moral code.

PAGE **138,** l. 3. *the death of Socrates*, in 399 B.C.

PAGE **140,** l. 32. *consumes the scabbard*, the moral fashions or codes of the age.

PAGE **142**, l. 6. *The bucolic writers*, Theocritus was born in Syracuse, perhaps in 315 B.C., seven years after the classic age ended with the death of Demosthenes, perhaps in one of the early decades of the next century. He lived for a time in Alexandria, and wrote courtly poems to Ptolemy Philadelphus, and to Hiero, the tyrant of his native city. His followers, Bion and Moschus, lived in Alexandria.

PAGE **143**, l. 12. *Astraea*, daughter of Zeus and Themis, and identified with Dike or Justice, the last of the gods to leave mankind at the passing of the Golden Age.

PAGE **144**, l. 17. *quia carent vate sacro*, 'for that they have no inspired bard', Horace, IV *Odes*, ix. 28.

l. 23. *The principle of equality*, &c. Plato desired that the Guardians of his ideal state should have no private property, and should regard themselves as a single family. Much in Plato's thinking (e.g. aristocracy, asceticism, and the transmigration of souls) derived from Pythagoras, who flourished in the sixth century. In the *Timaeus* Plato ascribes to the Pythagorean philosopher of that name, a contemporary of Socrates, many of his guesses at physics and metaphysics.

PAGE **145,** l. 3. *Celtic,* for Germanic.

l. 26. *Galeotto fù il libro,* &c., 'a Gallehaut was the book and he who wrote it'. Francesca, in Dante's *Inferno,* v. 137, tells how Paolo declared his love for her as they read together the romance of Lancelot. Gallehaut was the intermediary between Lancelot and Guinevere.

PAGE **146,** l. 3. *Vita Nuova,* the narrative of his love for Beatrice, written about 1292.

l. 15. *a worthy poet in Plato alone,* especially in Agathon's praise of love in the *Symposium.*

PAGE **147,** l. 7. *Riphaeus, Aeneid,* ii. 426–8:

> cadit et Rhipeus, iustissimus unus
> qui fuit in Teucris et servantissimus aequi
> (dis aliter visum).

' Fallen too is Rhipeus, of all the men of Troy supremely just, supremely mindful of the right; the Gods' will was not as men's.'

His soul is placed in the Christian Heaven in the *Paradiso,* xx. 67 f.

PAGE **148,** l. 23. *the flock of mock-birds,* Apollonius Rhodius, born about 290 B.C., author of the *Argonautica;* Quintus Calaber, alias Quintus Smyrnaeus, author of *Posthomerica,* an epic poem on the events of the Trojan War after the death of Hector, written at the end of the fourth century A.D.; Nonnus, a Greek poet of the sixth century of our era, author of *Dionysiaca,* an epic in forty-eight books; Lucan, author of the *Pharsalia* (see note to *Adonais,* l. 404); Statius (A.D. 61–96), author of the *Thebais,* on the exploits of the Seven against Thebes; Claudian, author of epic poems on the wars of Stilicho against the Goths (*De Bello Getico*) and the Rape of Proserpine (*De Raptu Proserpinae*), at the end of the fourth century and after.

PAGE **150,** l. 3. '*It is better to go*', &c. Ecclesiastes, vii. 2.

PAGE **151,** l. 12. '*letting I dare not*', &c., *Macbeth,* I. vii. 44.

PAGE **153,** l. 6. *We have his own authority, Paradise Lost,* IX. 21 f.

PAGE **154,** l. 10. *it arrests the vanishing apparitions,* &c. The darkness between two moons corresponds with the periods of dulness. These are haunted by fading memories of the 'visitations of divinity', which the poet arrests and revives and sends forth in artistic form to other men. His readers are thereby enabled to recapture their own similar (or 'sister') experiences, but cannot, like the poet, let them out into the universe by expressing them.

l. 31. '*The mind is its own place*', &c. *Paradise Lost,* i. 254.

l. 34. *And whether it spreads its own figured curtain,* &c., i.e.

either masking what is undelightful in reality as by a figured curtain, or disclosing its hidden beauty, as by withdrawing a veil.

PAGE **155,** l. 3. *a being within our being,* see the essay *On Love.*
l. 12. *Non merita nome,* &c., 'none deserves the name of Creator but God and the poet', a saying of Tasso's.

PAGE **156.**   PREFACE TO ALASTOR
The good die first, &c., *The Excursion,* i. 520.

ON LOVE

PAGE **159,** l. 24. *Not only the portrait,* &c. To make a sentence, 'we dimly see' must be supplied from the foregoing. In the perfect and uninjured soul deep within him a man may see not only his ideal self as it is expressed in external action, but the sum of whatever in him is most purely spiritual. Shelley is using the language of Lucretius (iii. 177 f.), when he asserts that the soul, though material, is composed of superfine particles.

LETTER TO PEACOCK, JULY 12, 1816

PAGE **160.**   In June 1816 the Shelleys were tenanting a cottage close to Coligny, by Geneva, a short way from the Villa Diodati, where Byron was lodging. From 23 June to 1 July the two poets coasted the shores of the lake and landed at various places. This letter is an account of the voyage, which prompted Byron's *Prisoner of Chillon* and a part of the third canto of *Childe Harold.* Shelley buried himself in *La Nouvelle Héloïse* between his excursions into the scenery it has consecrated.

PAGE **161,** l. 28. 'It was on the third day, or rather night, of the 27th of June 1787, between the hours of eleven and twelve, that I wrote the last lines of the last page [of *The Decline and Fall*] in a summer-house in my garden [at Lausanne]. After laying down my pen I took several turns in a *berceau,* or covered walk of acacias, which commands a prospect of the country, the lake, and the mountains. The air was temperate, the sky was serene, the silver orb of the moon was reflected from the waters, and all nature was silent. I will not describe the first emotions of joy on the recovery of my freedom and, perhaps, the establishment of my fame. But my pride was soon humbled, and a sober melancholy was spread over my mind by the idea that I had taken an everlasting leave of an old and agreeable companion, and that, whatsoever might be the future date of my History, the life of the historian must be short and precarious' (from Gibbon's *Autobiography*).

PAGE **162.** LETTER TO PEACOCK, JULY 22 AND 24, 1816

This letter was written during an excursion made by Shelley, in company with his wife and Claire Clairmont, from their lake-side cottage, close to Coligny, by Geneva, to Chamouni and back, 20 to 27 July 1816.

PAGE **163,** l. 18. *Buffon's . . . theory*, Shelley was deeply interested in Buffon's *Histoire Naturelle* (1749–88).

l. 22. *you who assert the supremacy of Ahriman*, the Evil Principle of the Zoroastrian philosophy, opposed to Ormuzd, the Good Principle. Peacock had handled the theme in his poem, *Ahrimanes*.

PAGE **164.** TO PEACOCK, 9 NOVEMBER 1818

The St. Cecilia was seen by Shelley in the Academy of Fine Arts at Bologna, when he passed through the town in November 1818.

TO PEACOCK, 22 DECEMBER 1818

The amphitheatre of the Coliseum, begun by Vespasian, and completed by Titus in A.D. 80, seated at least 50,000 spectators and measured approximately 200 yards by 170, and in height 160 feet. The passages running round behind the seats were in four stories, and the 'piled arches' here mentioned were window openings. The place served as a fortress in the Middle Ages, and at the time of the Renaissance as a quarry for the stone of Roman palaces.

LETTER TO PEACOCK, 26 JANUARY 1819

PAGE **168,** l. 23. *upaithric*, under the open sky.

LETTER TO KEATS

The last period of Keats's fatal illness set in in April 1820. In the middle of September he sailed for Italy, and lingered out the last months of his life in Naples and Rome; where he died on 23 February 1821. He received Shelley's invitation (which he did not expressly decline) on 13 August, six weeks after the publication of the volume containing *Isabella, The Eve of St. Agnes*, and *Hyperion*.

PAGE **169,** footnote. *I am picked up*, &c., i.e. I have my place assigned to me; I am sorted out, and placed in my own poetic species.

TO THE EDITOR OF THE QUARTERLY

In April 1819 *The Revolt of Islam* was maliciously reviewed, and Shelley's personal character vilified, in *The Quarterly*. Shelley *contra mundum* was compared with Pharaoh in the Red Sea: 'Like the Egyptian of old the wheels of his chariot are broken; the path of mighty waters closes in upon him', &c. (see Dowden, *Life of Shelley*, ii. 300). He ascribed the article to Southey, and directly taxed him with it; but the author is now known to have been John Taylor Coleridge. William Gifford, satirist, critic, and scholar, was editor of *The Quarterly* from 1809 to 1824. On the review of *Endymion* see introductory note to *Adonais*.

PAGE **170**, l. 7. *there sitting*, &c. *Paradise Lost*, vi. 829.

PAGE **171**. TO MRS. SHELLEY, 9 AUGUST 1821

Shelley paid a visit to Byron at Ravenna from the 7th to the 17th of August 1821. The letter refers to the fifth canto of *Don Juan*, which was published in London, together with the third and fourth, in the course of these days (8 August). For nearly a year before this date Leigh Hunt had been ill and poor, and depended in part on Shelley's generosity. It was during this visit that Byron spontaneously suggested the plan of a liberal-minded Review, to be conducted by himself, Shelley, and Hunt; a design which, in the year following, brought Hunt to Italy and established him in the co-editorship of *The Liberal*.

TO PEACOCK, AUGUST 1821

PAGE **173**, l. 6. *a pamphlet signed John Bull*. Peacock, in a note, disclaims all acquaintance with this pamphlet.

l. 8. *Melincourt*, a novel by Peacock, published 1817.

TO JOHN GISBORNE

PAGE **174**, l. 9. *This earth*, &c., misquoted (and misunderstood) from the lines 'Oh pleasant exercise of hope and joy', published 1805, and afterwards in *The Prelude*, xi. 142–4.

l. 19. *Calderon*, Pedro C. de la Barca (1600–83), whose plays, and especially the religious dramas, or *Autos Sacramentales*, Shelley deeply admired, after being acquainted with them by Mrs. Gisborne. Cyprian is the hero of the *Magico Prodigioso*, of which Shelley translated some scenes in March 1822.

l. 24. *a paper for our journal, The Liberal*: Scene II of his translations from *Faust*—that of the *Walpurgisnacht* (see note *infra*)—was published in the first number.

l. 33. *etchings from a German master*, Moritz Retsch.

PAGE **175**, l. 3. *Walpurgisnacht*. St. Walburga, abbess of Heidenheim, was patron of magic arts. On the night preceding her festal day, 1 May, the Devil was supposed to dance with witches on the Blocksberg, or Brocken, the highest point of the Harz Mountains. The scene is that in which Faust takes part in the revel and sees the ghost of Margaret.